He 219

From High-speed Bomber to Night Fighter

The Prototypes

Joachim Dressel and Manfred Griehl

The He 219 V 1 (VG+LW) on approach to land. Photo: Held

In 1940 the Heinkel design bureau projected several versions of a twin-engined aircraft as a high-speed bomber (Project P 1056) and reconnaissance aircraft (P 1055). During the course of the year this was developed into a multi-place, high-altitude reconnaissance aircraft at the request of the RLM. According to Heinkel company documents, the P 1055 was to have been capable of reaching a speed of approximately 750 kph and a service ceiling of 9,800 meters. The project was later pursued as a "reconnoiterer" and "day bomber." November 1940 saw the emergence of a heavy fighter variant, as there was obviously "an urgent requirement" for such an aircraft. The machine was to have a defensive armament of up to eight guns and two fixed weapons. A heavily-armed escort fighter followed in early 1941 and then finally, in the summer of 1941, a night fighter was requested and developed.

The project received the designation He 219 in August of the same year. One month later a mockup of the cockpit was ready for inspection by the RLM, followed by a complete airframe mockup in November 1941. The final inspection of the mockup was completed on April 7, 1942. The delivery of blueprints for the prototypes and the fabrication of individual parts be-

The first prototype during flight trials. Photo: Fl e.V.

Cockpit section of an early prototype, still with provision for an aft-firing MG 131. Photo: Heinkel

gan at the same time. The components were completed by September and final assembly of the first prototype was able to begin. By this time the decision had been made to concentrate He 219 development in Vienna-Schwechat.

Following extensive ground testing, on November 6, 1942 company pilot Peter took the V 1 (VG+LW) into the air for the first time.

On account of Generalfeldmarschall Milch's skepticism regarding the modern night fighter, a comparative suitability test was arranged involving the He 219, the Ju 188 and the Me 410. As a result of this the Bf 110 was adopted as an immediate solution, the Ju 88 C-6 as an interim night fighter and the Ju 188 N as a provisional final solution. This was based on a comparison flight on January 3, 1943 involving a Ju 188 whose defensive armament and external bomb racks had been removed. The extensively-lightened Junkers machine proved to be 30 kph faster than the He 219. By January 15, 1942 the He 219 V 1 had made a total of 46 flights, totalling 30 hours and 40 minutes of flying time. The aircraft was test flown by Oberstleutnant Petersen, Flight Staff Engineers Böttcher, Beauvais and Neidhardt and Major Streib among others.

Tests revealed that the aircraft's performance in horizontal flight was about 15 kph less than the company had guaranteed. As well stability about the yaw axis was inadequate and there was some vibration in the area of the tail assembly.

Several days later, on January 10, the He 219 V 2 (GG+WG) took off on its maiden flight. By this time the V 1 had completed 46 flights, in the course of which its performance was assessed as good. In particular the testing of the machine by Major Streib on January 15 and his positive report to Göring led to the order to increase monthly production to 100 aircraft.

Final assembly of an He 219 A-0. Photo: Heinkel

The He 219 V 1 at Marienehe. Photo: Held

The He 219 V 1 at Rostock, in the foreground the He 177 V 15. Photo: Fl e.V.

Wreckage of the He 219 V 2. Photo: Heinkel.

It wasn't until March 1943, however, that the He 219 was cleared for service use, after the planned remotely-controlled defensive armament was dropped and the fuselage was lengthened. Lengthening the fuselage and enlarging the vertical tail surfaces eliminated the following problems:

- inadequate stability about the yaw axis
- vibration in the fuselage and tail surfaces
- major trim changes during activation of the landing flaps

Another comparison trial between the He 219 V 1 and the Ju 188 on March 25-26, 1943 led to better results. Oberst von Lossberg and Staff Engineers Friebel and Böttcher informed Generalfeldmarschall Milch and others that the maximum speed of the He 219 was between 25 and 40 kph higher than the Ju 188 and that from a production standpoint the He 219 would be one of the best and most modern of service aircraft. Production costs were estimated as less than those of the He 111 and two-thirds less than the Ju 188.

The prototypes V 7 through V 9 were sent to Venlo for front-line testing. They were followed by several Zero-Series (pre-production) aircraft beginning in July 1943. The He 219 V 9 flew the first combat sorties by the type in June 1943.

In the beginning, however, a fully-equipped He 219 Gruppe remained an illusion, as did the requested 2,000 He 219s or the rapid changeover from the Zero-Series to the He 219 A-2. Even after Heinkel's repeated requests for more skilled workers for series production – in August 1943 – it still proved impossible to achieve a production rate of even ten aircraft per month.

On September 17, 1943 Generalfeldmarschall Milch spoke out in favor of an acceleration in He 219 production in spite of this problem and his initial negative attitude toward the aircraft. However, as deliveries continued to be slow until the end of the year, it appeared that a halt in production might be imminent. In the end, however, Milch decided that Heinkel-South in Vienna should produce fifty He 219s monthly, while Heinkel-North in Rostock was to simultaneously construct fifty Ju 88 G night fighters per month. There was, however, no concentration of production on the modern and advanced He 219 as Kammhuber and Galland had vehemently demanded.

Finally, on May 25, 1944, Göring surprised his subordinate by ordering that production of the He 219 was to be halted in favor of the Ju 388, even though the crews of the Heinkel night fighter were enjoying great success in combat. At the same time production and service testing continued at Schwechat and Venlo respectively. By now the first examples of the He 219 A-5 were available and its armament and performance were convincing. As a result, on June 13 Göring reversed his earlier deci-

Front view of the He 219 V 5. Photo: Heinkel.

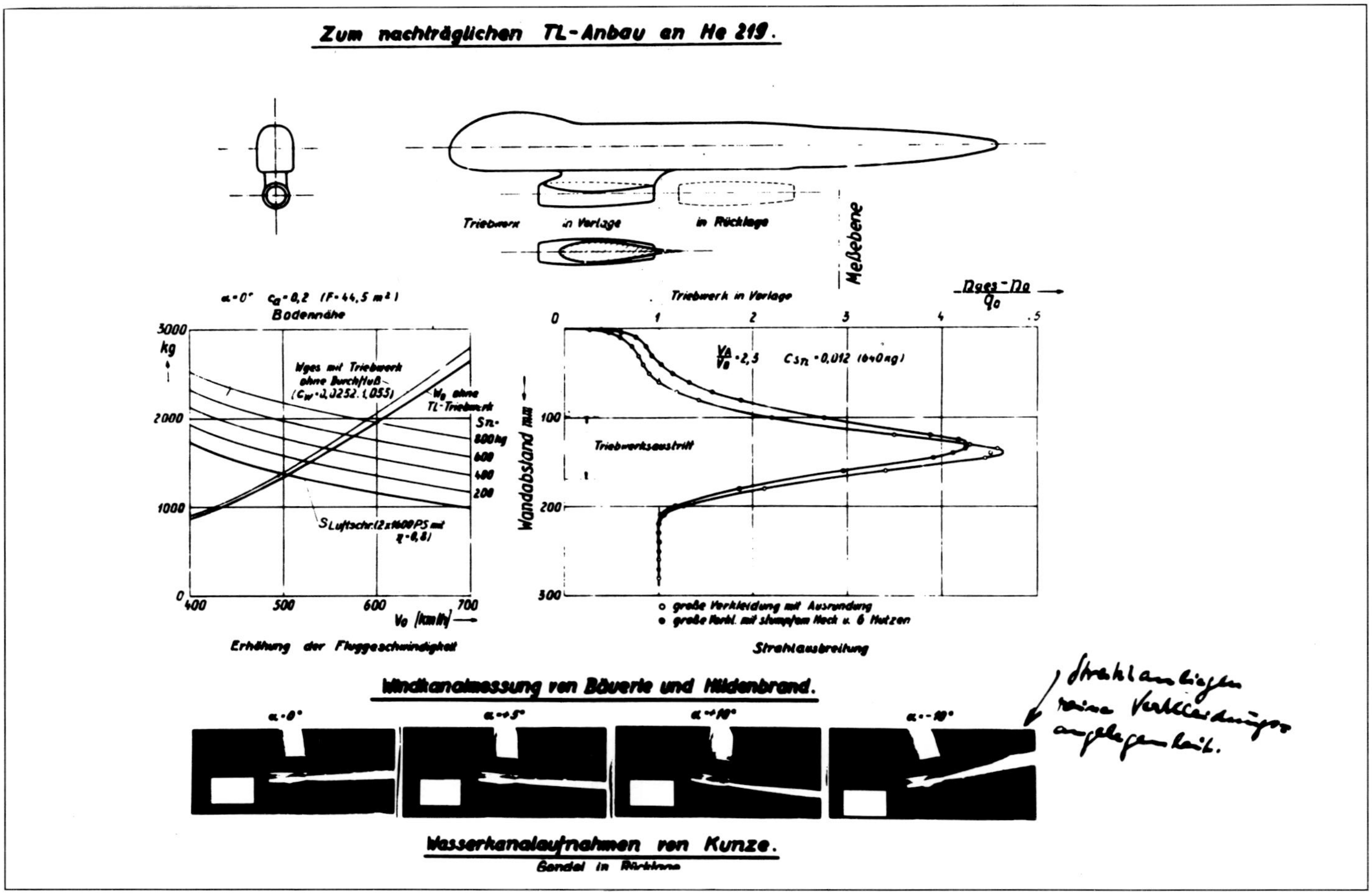

Above: An original page from the report on the installation of a BMW 003 jet engine, an attempt to obtain increased performance.

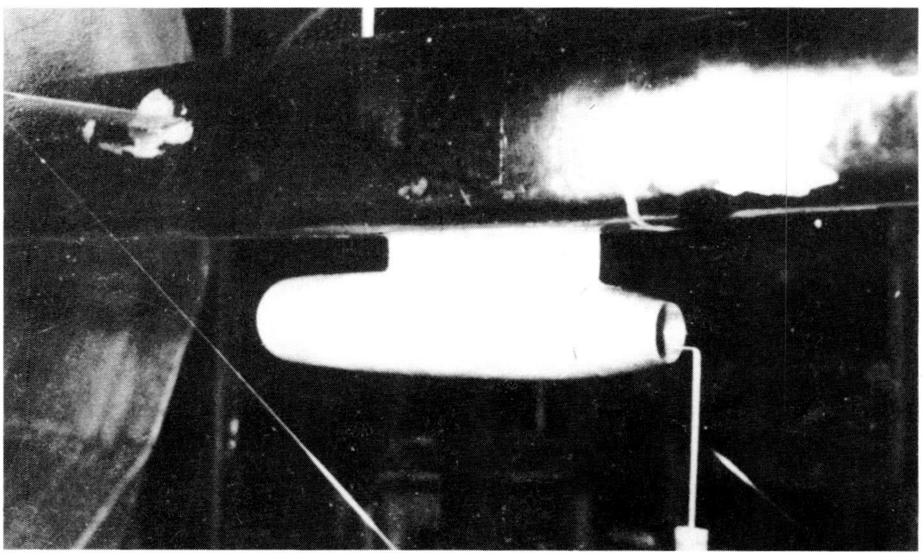

Left: A wind tunnel model of an He 219 fuselage with underslung jet engine. Griehl.

sion. Nevertheless, authorization for an increase in production from 50 to 150 aircraft per month was not forthcoming.

The He 219 enjoyed an excellent reputation among the crews of I/NJG 1 based at Venlo (commander Hauptmann Meurer). It was clearly preferred to the Me 110 and the Ju 88. The crews especially valued the type's increased endurance. In the course of "Wild Boar" missions crews were able to take off from Venlo and fly to Munich or the Hannover-Rostock-Stettin area and then return to base. This was especially important, because in autumn 1943 aircraft-specific servicing for the He 219 was available only at Venlo.

Changes were made to the type's planned armament on account of shortages of the MK 103 and MK 108 cannon. Increasingly the MG 151, which was readily available, was substituted for the large-caliber weapons.

True to life drawing of the jet-boosted prototype by H. Heumann.

The nosewheel of the He 219. Photo: Heinkel.

Rear view of the He 219's main undercarriage. Photo: Heinkel.

The first He 219 A-7 was handed over for front-line testing in July 1944. Apart from prototypes and mockups the B- and C-Series progressed no farther than the planning stage. The He 219 D and E got no farther than the drawing board.

Worthy of note are the He 219 V 18 with four-bladed propellers and Jumo 222A/B engines and the He 219 V 28 (VO+BC) and V 31 (DV+DB) with braking chute (tactical speed brake). Ejector seat trials were carried out with the He 219 V 6 and these were later continued with He 219 Werknummer 190113 (DV+DI). The crews of NJG 1 were at first highly skeptical about the use of the ejector seat. On November 19, 1942 General Kammhuber himself took part in a test, which involved being fired to a height of four meters at 6 G, in order to gain an impression of the Heinkel ejector seat.

The prototypes appeared in a variety of guises. For example, the He 219 V 16 was first modified to A-0/R6 and then to A-5 standard, the latter incorporating an SN-2 airborne radar. In the end this aircraft, like the V 19, was said to have been

Flying test bed for ejector seat trials. Photo: Creek

Taken from an instructional manual, a photograph of the He 219's internal armor-glass windscreen. Note the folded-down armored visor in front of the gunsight. Photo: Heinkel

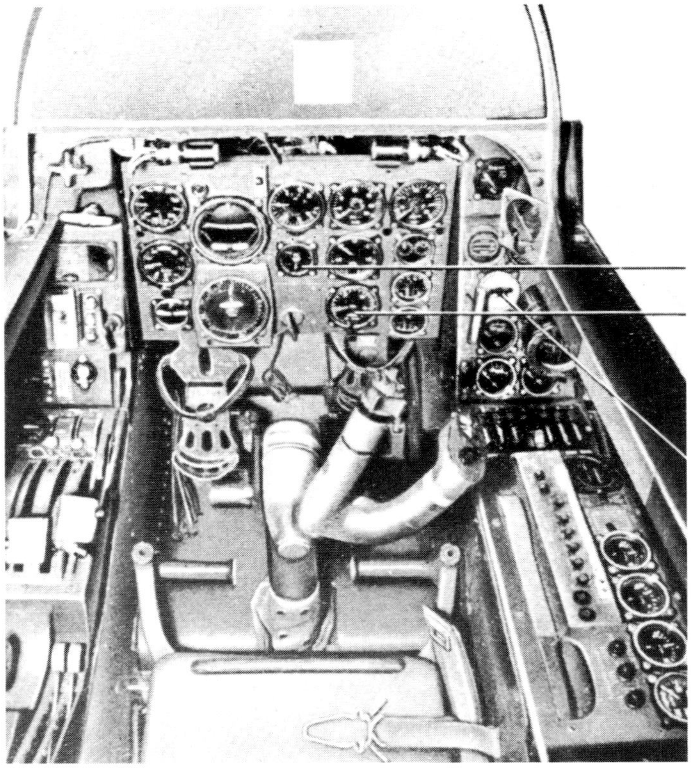

View of the instrument panel and side consoles of the He 219 A-0. Photo: Heinkel

handed over to NJG 1 equipped with oblique-firing armament.

The V 28 (RL+AH) was the forerunner of the He 219 A-5/R3. The machine arrived in Venlo in June 1944. The V 22 served as a flying test bed for the DB 603 G. In July 1944 the V 25 flew as the three-seat A-5/R4.

The same month Director Francke announced the results of performance testing:

The maximum speed of the He 219 equipped with DB 603 A engines, SN-2 antennas and flame dampers was 585 kph. Heinkel hoped to achieve a further increase in performance through the installation of more powerful engines, however Jumo failed to develop the Jumo 222 to production standard, while both the DB 603 L and Jumo 213 with MW 50 boost continued to present problems.

With the Jumo 222 A/B the He 219 could have attained a maximum speed of 620 kph at 7,500 meters. A combination of the Jumo 222 E/F and an improved Lichtenstein array would have increased maximum speed by 46 kph at maximum boost altitude. It was hoped that with this power plant a further five-percent increase in performance would be achieved through the use of methanol-water injection, but only at high altitude. Powered by the Jumo 213 E, which was derived from the standard A-2 engine, the He 219 was capable

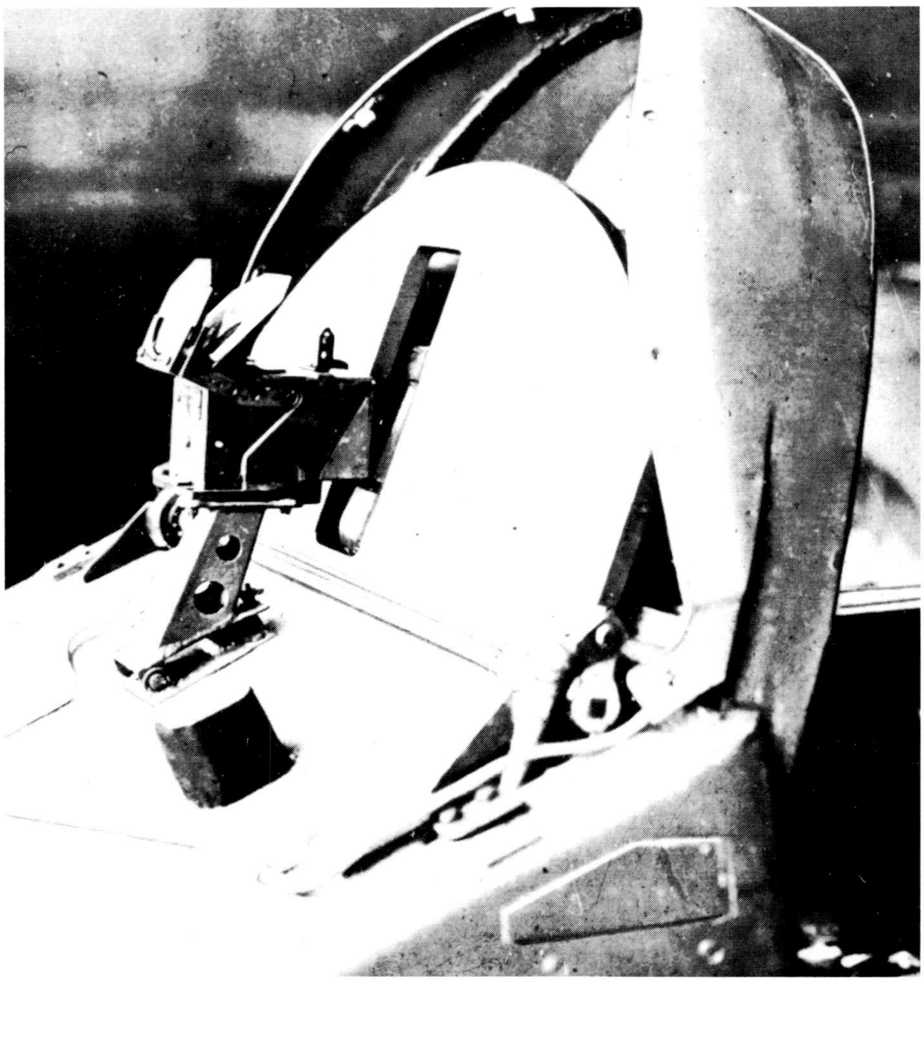

Folding armored visor with cutout for the Revi 16 gunsight. Photo: Heinkel

Fragments of the He 219 V 11 at Vienna-Schwechat. Photo: Heinkel

The remains of a DB 603 with flame damper. Photo: Heinkel

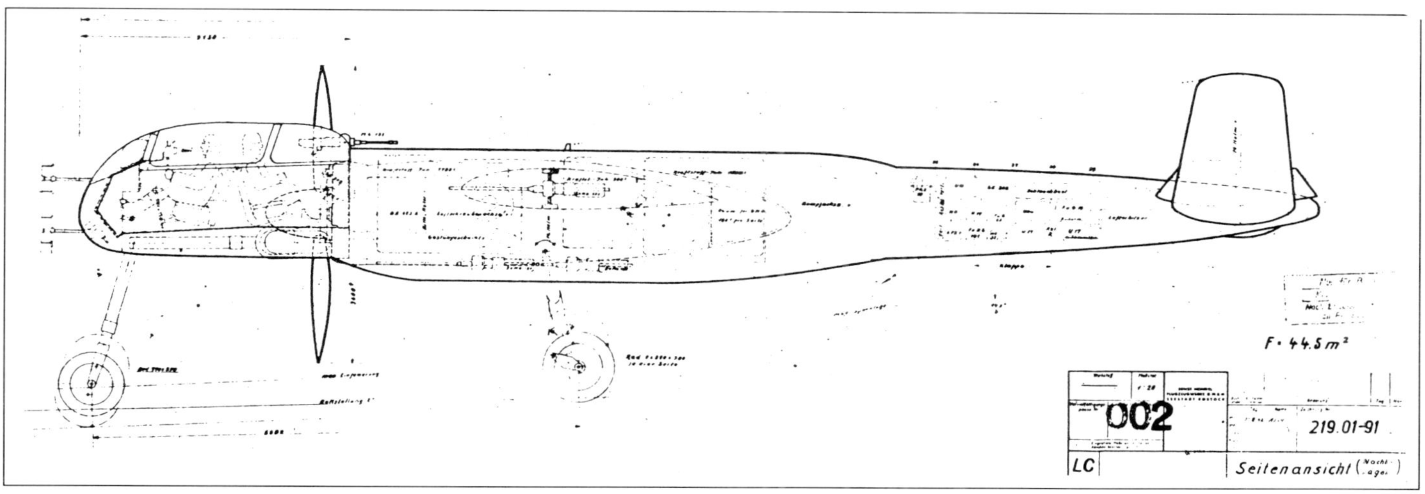

Side view of the He 219. Photo: Griehl

of 635 kph at 10,500 meters, 605 kph without methanol-water injection. However installation of the engine required extensive redesign in the area of the engine block, cowling, exhaust and lubrication systems and fire wall attachment points. Junkers ran into difficulties with the supercharger and only six aircraft were converted to the Jumo 213 E with MW 50 by the end of 1944. The problem persisted and even at the beginning of 1945 the type's service debut was still in the future due to overloading of the supercharger drive elements. Without the use of methanol-water injection performance was not significantly better than with the DB 603 and the He 219 was therefore never capable of attaining "Mosquito speeds."

The He 219 V 1 in flight over Marienehe. Photo: Griehl

From High-speed Bomber to Night Fighter

The He 219 A-5/R1 (DV/R1) at Munich-Riem in the summer of 1944. Photo: Bekker

The first part of the He 219 story provided an overview of the prototypes. What follows is a description of the most important service variants. In the period from 1943 until March 1945 Heinkel completed 268 He 219s as so-called "new construction aircraft." As well, six aircraft were constructed from surplus spare parts. More than 27 night fighters were repaired following in some cases major damage and were returned to NJG 1. The front-line units, mainly NJG 1, received only 195 He 219s. The rest were used for test purposes or were lost through enemy action. Forty-six He 219s were written off as total losses and more than 17 were seriously damaged.

An He 219 A-0 of NJGr 10 at Rechlin. Photo: Thiele

He 219 Prototypes

(as of March 14, 1944, EHAG)

Aircraft	Werk-nummer	Test Missions
V 1	000 001	Handling tests, stall tests
V 2	000 002	Diving flights
V 3	190 003	Engine, fuel jettisoning, warm water heating trials, new undercarriage, pedal steering and lengthened cockpit glazing
V 4	190 004	Power plant tests
V 5	190 005	Weapons testing, prototype MK 108 installation
V 6	190 006	Ejector seat trials and radio equipment testing
V 7	190 007	Operational aircraft
V 8	190 008	Undercarriage testing
V 9	190 009	Operational aircraft
V 10	190 010	Operational aircraft
V 11	190 011	Diving flights (safety parachute and electrical tailplane trimming)
V 12	190 012	Operational aircraft
A-0/V 13	190 052	Testing of fuel jettisoning and warm water heating, lengthened cockpit glazing
A-0/V 14	190 058	Performance increase and vertical stabilizer tests
A-0/V 15	190 064	Prototype GM-1 system installation, installation and testing of FuG 16ZY
A-0/V 16	190 192	Prototype Jumo 222 A/B installation, lengthened wings and larger wheels
A-0/V 17	190 060	Operational aircraft with G-supercharger, "anti-Mosquito" trials
A-0/V 18	190 071	Prototype installation of six MK 108 cannon in ventral tray
A-0/V 19		Planned 1st prototype pressurized cockpit
A-0/V 20		Planned 2nd prototype pressurized cockpit
A-0/V 21	190 117	1st prototype DB 603 A standard engine
A-0/V 22		2nd prototype DB 603 G standard engine
A-0/V 23		2nd prototype with Jumo 222 A/B, lengthened wings and larger wheels
A-0/V 24		Prototype installation of two MK 103 cannon under the fuselage as well as possible installation of BMW jet engine
A-0/V 25	190 122	Prototype installation of single-conductor cable for radio gear and electrical equipment (simplified electronics)
A-0/V 26	190 120	Obliquely-mounted MK 108 in fuselage behind Frame 20
A-0/V 27		Prototype for B-1 series, flattened canopy and miniaturized standard equipment
A-0/V 28	190 068	Duration trials with DB 603 E engine and testing of tactical brake (braking parachute trials)
A-0/V 29	190 069	De-icing and heating tests (warmwater heating)
A-0/V 30	190 101	2nd prototype with BMW jet engine under fuselage
A-0/V 31	190 106	Operational aircraft; also structural strength test flights
A-0/V 32	190 121	2nd prototype with GM-1 system, miniaturized standard equipment
A-0/V 33	190 063	Installation of parabolic reflector (antenna test bed)
A-0/V 34	190 112	Prototype three-man cockpit, oblique armament, increased range and MG 131 (hand-operated) in cockpit

Operational aircraft of 1/NJG 1 at Westerland, Sylt. Photo: Franklin

Production output of the He 219 was distributed as follows:

1st-4th quarters 1943:	11 aircraft
1st quarter 1944:	27 aircraft
2nd quarter 1944:	55 aircraft
3rd quarter 1944:	50 aircraft
4th quarter 1944:	63 aircraft
1st quarter 1945:	62 aircraft

6 aircraft from replacement parts

Werknummern were assigned as follows:

190 000 prototypes and Zero-Series (pre-production)
190 100 prototypes and Zero-Series
190 200 prototypes and Zero-Series
290 000 A-2 series
290 100 A-2 series
290 200 A-2 series
310 300 A-2 series
310 000 A-7 series
310 100 A-7 series

With more than 100 built, the A-0 was the most-produced variant of the He 219. Different versions of the A-0 appeared with diverse modifications; these were reflected in Rüstsatz (R) designations, because a new designation, for example A-1 or A-2, was not chosen as was usual practice. For details refer to the table "Summary of He 219 Variants." As well there existed various weapons modification kits which were identified by the abbreviation "M":

M1: 2 x MG 151/15 and 4 x MK 108
M2: 4 x MK 103 in the ventral weapons tray
M3: 2 x MG 151/15 and 4 x MK 103

The He 219 A-2 saw action in noteworthy numbers as a long-range night fighter. 210 examples of the A-7 variant were to have been built between December 1944 and July 1945 (according to the plan dated December 22, 1944). The first five of these machines were fitted with the DB 603 A and the rest with the more powerful DB 603 E, however only a relatively small number of A-7s were completed.

The prototype installation of a BMW 003 jet engine beneath the fuselage of an He 219 A-0 was carried out in the summer of 1943. According to calculations by the Göttingen Aerodynamic Research Institute, at idle the jet engine should have produced a loss in speed of only 10 kph while providing an increase in speed of 60 kph while operating at a thrust level of 6.37kN. Wind tunnel tests were almost complete by November 1943.

An He 219 on a delivery flight from Rostock to NJG 1 in Venlo. Photo: Petrick

The He 219 A-5/R1, formerly an A-0/R6, equipped with FuG 212 and FuG 220 radars. Photo: Bekker

The first flight (He 219 A-010), with the jet engine at idle, took place on September 23, 1943. Soon afterward speeds of 530 kph were achieved at a height of approximately 50 meters with the BMW 003 engine running. The prototype crashed in the course of a speed test flight on November 13, 1943. The appearance of flames from the jet exhaust convinced the crew that the aircraft was on fire. After both piston engines failed the crew made a forced landing at Aspern (40% damage). The conversion of a second He 219 to auxiliary jet power began in January 1944 but had not been completed by April of the same year. Testing with the V 30 was then halted in the summer.

Heinkel projected a series of variants to succeed the A-Series, however none proceeded farther than the mockup or prototype stage. The designers planned the

Summary of He 219 Variants

Designation	Type	Power Plants	Armament	Radar Equipment
A-0/R1	Lengthened fuselage compared to prototypes, standard wing,	DB 603 A	2 MK 108 in ventral tray, 2 MG 151 in wing roots, weapons modification kits M1-M3	FuG 212 C1
A-0/R2	similar to A-0/R1, strengthened undercarriage	DB 603 A	4 MK 103 in ventral tray	FuG 212 C1
A-0/R3	Prototype for A-2 series (improved A-0)	DB 603 A	4 MK 103 in ventral tray, 2 MG 151 in wing roots	FuG 212 C2
A-0/R6	Prototype for A-5 series	DB 603 A	4 MK 108 in ventral tray, 2 MG 151 in wing roots, 2 obliquely-mounted MK 108 in fuselage,	FuG 212 and 220
A-1	Planned production version of A-0, flattened canopy over two-man cockpit	DB 603 A/B	Weapons modification kits M1-M3	
A-2/R1	Improved A-0, single-conductor cable layout, two-man cockpit, increased range	DB 603 A/B	2 MK 103 in ventral tray, 2 MG 151 in wing roots, 2 obliquely-mounted MK 108 in fuselage	FuG 220
A-2/R2	similar to A-2/R1, flame damper tests, development of A-2 with 900-liter external tanks and miniaturized standard equipment, two-man cockpit, planned as bomber	DB 603 A/B, DB 603 E/F,G DB 603	as A-2/R1, 2 MK 108 in wing roots, oblique armament planned	FuG 220
A-4	development of A-2 for anti-Mosquito and reconnaissance roles, reduced armor and weapons, GM-1 and ejector exhausts, two-man cockpit	DB 603 A/B,2 Jumo 222 2	MK 108 in wing roots, MK 103 in ventral tray	
A-5/R1	Development of the A-3, previous designation A-0/R6	DB 603 A	2 MG 151 in wing roots, 2 MK 108 in ventral tray, 2 obliquely-mounted MK 108 in fuselage	FuG 212 and 220
A-5/R2	Forerunner of A-7/R4	DB 603 A	2 MG 151 in wing roots, 2 MG 151 in ventral tray, 2 obliquely-mounted MK 108 in fuselage	FuG 220
A-5/R3	Production version based on the He 219 V 28	DB 603 E	2 MG 151 in wing roots, 2 MK 103 in ventral tray, 2 obliquely-mounted MK 108 in fuselage	FuG 220
A-5/R4	Development of the A-3 with three-man cockpit, increased range and defensive armament based on the He 219 V 34	DB 603 E	2 MG 151 in wing roots, 2 MG 151 in ventral tray, 2 obliquely-mounted MK 108 in fuselage, defensive armament in cockpit possible	FuG 220
A-6	Unarmored version of the He 219 A-2	DB 603 E	2 MG 151 in wing roots, 2 MG 151 in ventral tray	FuG 220
A-7/R1	Improved production variant based on the He 219 V 26 2	DB 603 G	2 MK 108 in wing roots, MG 151 and 2 MK 103 in ventral tray	FuG 220
A-7/R2	Production version with oblique armament, prototype: He 219 V 26	DB 603 G	Armament similar to A-7/R1 but with 2 obliquely-mounted MK 108	FuG 220
A-7/R3	Pre-production series for planned B-1 series, prototype: He 219 V 27	DB 603 G	2 MG 151 in wing roots, 2 MG 151 in ventral tray, 2 obliquely-mounted MK 108 in fuselage	FuG 220
A-7/R4	Variant with reduced armament	DB 603 G	2 MG 151 in wing roots, 2 MG 151 in ventral tray	FuG 220
A-7/R5	Mosquito hunter with MW50 system	Jumo 213 E	2 MG 151 in wing roots, 2 MG 151 in ventral tray	
A-7/R6	Testbed for Jumo 222 A, prototype: He 219 V 18	Jumo 222 A	2 MG 151 in wing roots, 4 MK 108 in ventral tray	

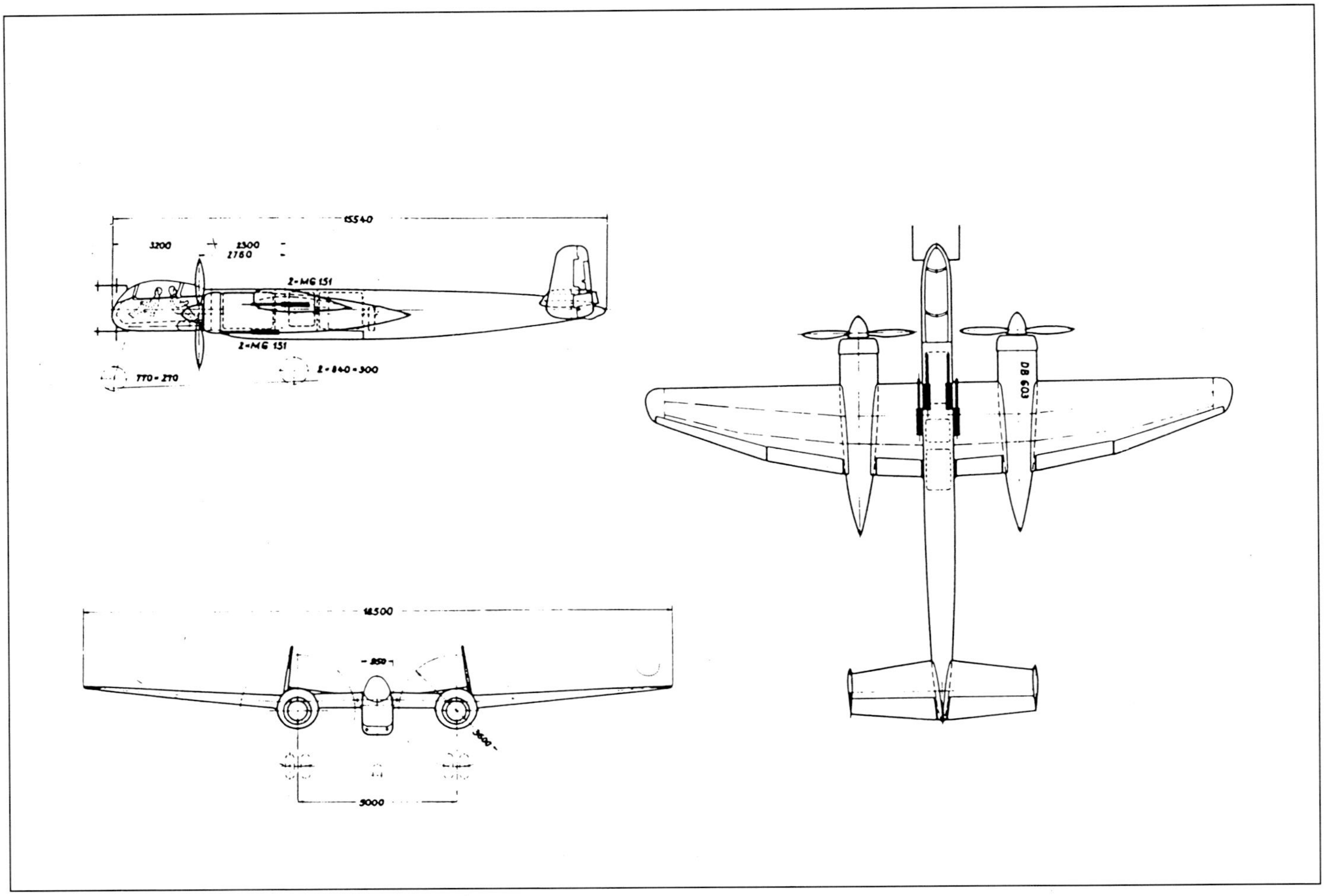

A three-view drawing of the He 219 A-6 Mosquito hunter, which featured a reduced armament. Photo: Heinkel

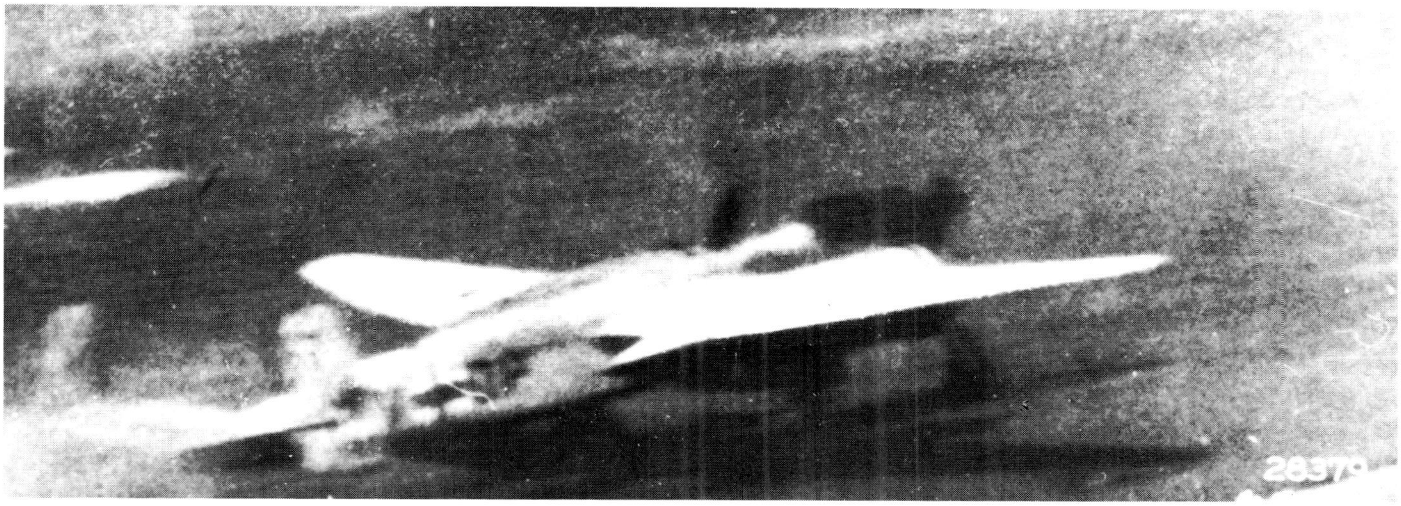

NJG 1's base under attack by American long-range fighters. Photo: USAF

He 219 photographed at Bindach near Bayreuth, early 1945. Photo: USAF

He 219s destroyed in an air attack on the factory prior to delivery. Photo: Heinkel.

two-seat He 219 B-1 as a major production series; powered by the Jumo 222 A/B, it incorporated a flattened cockpit canopy, wing fuel tanks for increased range, a strengthened undercarriage and an increased wingspan of 22 meters. Armament of the B-1, which was to have expanded equipment for the night-fighter role, was to consist of two MG 151 cannon in the fuselage, two in the wing roots and two obliquely-mounted MK 108 cannon.

The three-seat He 219 B-2 was a planned development of the B-1. Apart from the use of Jumo 222 E/F engines, the B-2 differed from its predecessor through the addition of auxiliary fuel tanks, a larger nosewheel and a revised armament (2 MK 108 cannon in the wing roots and two mounted obliquely in the fuselage). No ventral weapons tray was planned. A prototype of the B-2 made its first flight on June 5, 1944. Testing revealed a maximum speed of 700 kph; the aircraft also exhibited minor instability in flight.

The He 219 C-1 was a heavily-armed development which was to have received an HL 131 V dorsal turret with four MG 131 machine-guns in addition to the fixed armament of the B-2. The fuselage of this three-seat night fighter was to have been lengthened by 1 meter between Frames 9 and 10 and the Jumo 222 E/F engines moved forward by .30 meters.

Heinkel designed the He 219 C-2 as a "multi-role aircraft." The fuselage was similar to that of the C-1, however the oblique armament was dropped. A revised fuel tank arrangement allowed an additional 450 liters of fuel to be carried. Proposed armament was two MK 103 cannon on the fuselage sides beside the cockpit as well as the HL 131 V dorsal turret. Provision was also to have been made for racks for loads of up to 1,500 kilograms of bombs.

Like other versions in the B- and C-Series, the end of the war precluded series production.

The severed cockpit section of Oberleutnant Werner Streib's He 219 A-0.

The He 219 in Action

The He 219 night fighter proved extremely effective in spite of the relatively small number of machines that saw action. Altogether He 219 crews reported 111 enemy aircraft destroyed in the period from June 12, 1943 to June 25, 1944.

The first operational unit with He 219s was NJG 1 in Venlo. This unit had earlier received the prototypes V 7 to V 9 for operational testing in May 1943 (as part of XII Fliegerkorps).

On June 12, 1943 Major (later Oberstleutnant) Streib was able to shoot down five enemy aircraft flying G9+FB. Following the delivery of further He 219s to I/NJG 1, the unit's commander, Hauptmann Frank, was successful with his He 219 G9+CB. After Frank died in a collision with another night fighter on September 27, Hauptmann Meurer became the new commander of the Gruppe. After achieving 65 victories, including five with the He 219, at the end of January 1944 Meurer collided with a British bomber and died in the wreckage of his He 219 G9+BB. Hauptmann Förster subsequently took command of I/NJG 1. On October 1, 1944 Förster crashed near Handorf while on a test flight. Hauptmann Werner Baake was named new Gruppe commander. Baake led I/NJG 1, which in September 1944 was forced by the Allied advance to move from Venlo to Handorf near Münster and then to the Düsseldorf area, until the end of the war.

II/NJG 1 was also forced to move its night fighters from Deelen near Arnheim to Düsseldorf in autumn 1944. 2nd Staffel of I Gruppe flew from Mendig for a time. In November 1944 the Geschwaderstab of NJG 1 (Bf 110 G-4) and the embryonic Stabsstaffel (Bf 110 G-4 and He 219 A) as well as a small detachment from II/NJG 1 were located in Paderborn.

The commander of I/NJG 1, Hauptmann Förster, in front of an He 219. Photo: Heinkel.

Streib's He 219 A-0 (G9+FB), which crashed on account of an instrument failure and a landing flaps malfunction.

The Gruppenstab of I/NJG 1 and the 1st and 3rd Staffeln continued to operate from Münster-Handorf. Also based there as of December 1944 was the Einsatzstaffel Lukesch with the Ar 234s of 9/KG 76. The rest of II Gruppe, which was equipped with the Bf 110, was located at bases in the Fritzlar area with a detachment near Giessen.

At the beginning of 1945 the Stabsstaffel was built up to a strength of about 30 (!) He 219s and Bf 110s. All remaining aircraft were concentrated in I/NJG 1 for maintenance reasons. While the Stabsstaffel was under the command of the 1st Fighter Division, the Stab and the four Gruppen were attached to the 3rd Fighter Division. As of April 1945 the entire Geschwader was commanded by 1st Fighter Division. Simultaneously NJG 1 was forced to merge the He 219-equipped 1st-3rd Staffeln into a single operational Staffel. The same was done with the three Bf 110 G-equipped Gruppen. The result was three Staffeln designated 4, 7 and 10 (Einsatz)/NJG 1, which were based in Westerland and on the island of Sylt.

Three months earlier, on January 10, 1945, I/NJG 1 had an actual strength of 64 He 219s, of which 45 were serviceable. On April 11 the remaining elements of NJG 1 also transferred to Schleswig, Husum or Sylt. The last base of the Geschwaderstab was in Eggebeck, Schleswig. In spite of the difficult situation the unit nevertheless succeeded in putting as many as sixteen He 219 night fighters into the air in one day.

He 219 A with FuG 212 and FuG 220 photographed at Rechlin-Lärz in the summer of 1944 during equipment testing. Photo: Thiele

He 219 A-5/R2 (Werknummer 310189) was captured by British troops in Schleswig in April 1945. In addition to this aircraft, after the war the RAE and RAF also tested Werknummern 290126, 310106, 310109 and 310215, all He 219 A-2s. Photo: Franklin

He 219, Baureihe:		A-2		A-5	B-1		C-1		C-2	A-6		B-2
Kennzeichen:		2-Mann-Jäger: Serien-überarbeitete Erstausführung, Schrägbewaffnung, Zusatzkraftstoff.		3-Mann-Jäger: Weiterentwicklung A2 3-Mann, Gondelzusatzkraftstoff, grössere Volldruckhöhe (603E)	3-Mann-Jäger Leistungssteigerung durch JUMO 222, grosse Fläche, Gondelzusatzkraftstoff.		4-Mann-Jäger: Weiterentwicklung durch bemannt. Heckstand, Waffen-Besatzungsneuanordnung.		4-Mann-Jagdbomber: Abwurfanlage, Heckstand 4x131, Bewaffnung MK 103	Mosquito-Jäger: A-2 erleichtert in Triebwerk-Munitionspanzer, Schrägbewaffnung entfällt.		Höhenjäger: Druckkanzel 2-Mann, Höhenmotor gr. Fläche, erleichtert wie A-4.
Fläche-Spannweite	m^2 m	44,5 - 18,5			50 - 22					44.5 - 18.5		50 - 22
Bewaffnung:		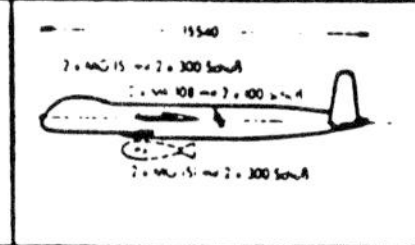		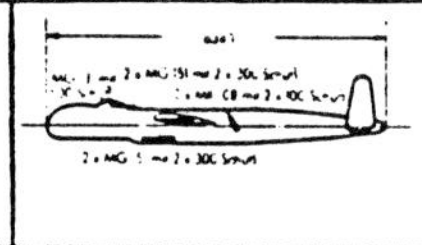	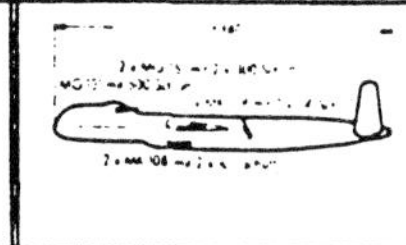		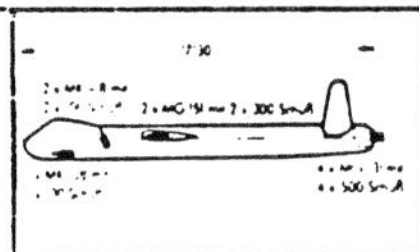		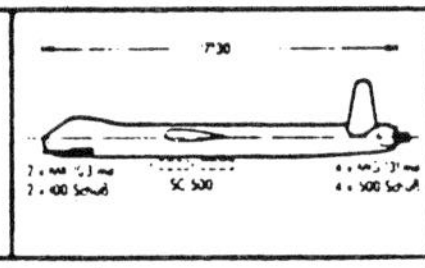	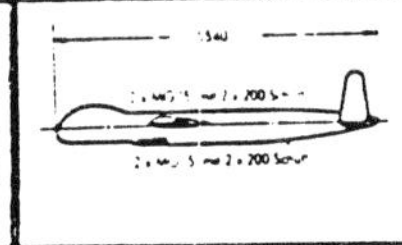		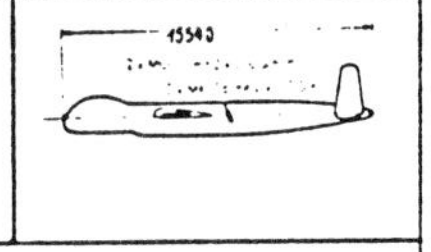
Kanzel:		2 - Mann		3 - Mann hintereinander	3 - Mann hintereinander		Arbeitskanzel 3-Mann gestaffelt nebeneinander			2-Mann		
Haupträder Bugrad	mm mm	840 x 300 770 x 270		840 x 300 770 x 270	935 x 345 770 x 270		935 x 345 935 x 345			840 x 300 770 x 270		
FT - Anlage:		FuG 16 ZY, FuG 10 P, FuG 25 A FuG 101 A, FuG 220, FuBl 2 F		Wie A-2 mit Radione	FuG 15, FuG 10 P, FuG 25 A FuG 101 A, FuG 220, FuBl.2 F Radione				FuG 15, FuG 10 P, FuG 101 A FuG 25 A, FuG 104, FuBl.2 F	FuG 16, FuG 10 P, FuBl 2F FuG 101, FuG 220, FuG 25		FuG 15, FuG 10 P, FuBl 2F FuG 101 A, FuG 220, FuG 25
Kraftstoffbehälter:		2600 l im Rumpf 900 l abwerfbar.		2600 l im Rumpf 780 l in Motorgondel	2600 l im Rumpf 1200 l in Mot.Gond.		3050 l im Rumpf 800 l im Flügel			2600 l im Rumpf		
Triebwerk:		DB 603 A		DB 603 E	222 A/B-3	JUMO 222 E/F	222 A/B-3	JUMO 222 E/F	JUMO 222 E/F	DB-603 E	DB 603 L	DB 603 mit Abgaslad.
Startleistung	PS	1750		1800	2500	2500	2500	2500	2500	1750	1750	1700
Kampfleistung Volldr.	PS	1510		1380	1980	1680	1980	1680	1680	1380	1420	1400
Volldruckhöhe	km	5,7		7,4	6,4	10,9	6,4	10,9	10,9	7.4	9	13
Leergewicht	kg	8120	8250	8345	9511	9846	9706	10054	9990	8150	8300	9300
Besatzung	kg	200	200	300	300	300	400	400	400	200	200	200
Schusswaffen	kg	518	518	558	537	537	963	963	911	250	250	342
Munition	kg	385	385	428	411	411	536	536	392	179	179	207
Panzerung	kg	390	390	390	195	195	250	250	150	134	134	134
Ausrüstung (o. Waff.)	kg	802	809	834	791	791	805	805	847	802	802	802
Abwurfslast	kg	-	-	-	-	-	-	-	1500	-	-	-
Kraftstoff, normal	kg	1925	1925	2505	2815	2815	2850	2850	2850	1925	1925	1925
Zusatzkraftstoff	kg	-	665	-	-	-	-	-	-	-	-	-
Schmierstoff	kg	160	215	215	240	240	240	240	240	160	160	160
mil. Last	kg	2295	2302	2510	2234	2234	2954	2954	4200	1565	1565	1685
Abfluggewicht	kg	12500	13302	13575	14800	15135	15750	16085	17280	11800	11950	13070
Flügelfestigkeit b.G_m		6,3	6,0	5,9	5,1	5,0	4,7	4,6	4,2			
Flugleistungen:		o h n e Flammenvernichter - o h n e Suchantenne										
Höchstgeschwindigkeit in 0 m	km/h	500		490	530	510	515	490	505 (ohne Bomben)	500	500	465
in Volldr.-Höhe	km/h	605		615	655	705	630	675	690	630	650	655
Volldr.-Höhe m.Stau	km	6,4		8,4	7,4	11,7	7,3	11,6	11,7	8,6	10,2	13,0
Gr. Flugdauer/Strecke	h-km	4,8/2150	6,4/2850	6,3/2850	5,6/2550	3,8/2000	5,3/2350	3,6/1800	3,5/1800			
Mittl. Geschwindigkeit	km/h	455	445	455	560	525	450	505	510			
in Flughöhe	km	6,0	6,0	7,5	7,0	11,0	7,0	11,0	11,0			
Flugdauer/Strecke (mit max. Dauerl.)	h-km	2,7/1550	3,7/2100	3,6/2100	2,9/1800	2,9/1850	2,9/1700	2,9/1700	2,9/1700	3,4/1700	2,8/1600	2,4/1400
Mittl. Geschwindigk.	km/h	585	575	585	630	645	600	610	590	580	630	655
in Flughöhe	km	6,0	6,0	7,5	8,3	11,0	8,2	11,0	11,0	10,0	11,0	13,0
Dienstgipfelhöhe b.G_m	km	9,3	8,9	9,4	9,7	12,4	9,5	12,0	12,1	10,3	11,8	13,4
Rollweg beim Start	m	680	800	750	620	600	700	650	750	550	570	750
Startstrecke b. 20m Höh.	m	970	1120	1050	830	850	980	950	1100	850	880	1050
Flugleistungen:		m i t Flammenvernichter - m i t Suchantenne										
Höchstgeschwindigkeit in 0 m	km/h	460		450	505	485	490	460		475	475	465
in Volldr.-Höhe	km/h	560		585	620	650	595	615		600	615	655
Volldr.-Höhe m.Stau	km	6,3		8,3	7,2	11,4	7,1	11,2		8,5	10,0	13,0
Gr. Flugdauer/Strecke	h-km	4,8/1950	6,4/2550	6,3/2650	5,6/2400	3,2/1700	5,6/2350	3,1/1550				
Mittl. Geschwindigkeit	km/h	540	530	555	595	580	565	525				
in Flughöhe	km	6,0	6,0	7,5	7,0	11,0	7,0	11,0				
Flugdauer/Strecke (mit max. Dauerl.)	h-km	2,7/1450	3,7/1950	3,6/2000	2,9/1700	2,9/1650	2,9/1650	2,9/1500		3,4/1600	2,8/1500	2,4/1400
Mittl. Geschwindigk.	km/h	540	530	555	595	580	565	525		555	595	655
in Flughöhe	km	6,0	6,0	7,5	8,3	11,0	8,3	11,0		9,5	11,0	13,0
Dienstgipfelhöhe b.G_m	km	8,9	8,5	9,0	9,2	11,9	9,0	11,5		9,9	11,4	13,4

Bl. 13.

Table listing variants of the He 219.

Victories by I/NJG 1 with the He 219

Date	Name of Pilot	Number of Victories
12.06.1943	Major Streib	5
26.07.1943	Hptm. Frank	2
23.08.1943	Hptm. Frank	1
31.08.1943	Hptm. Frank	3
06.09.1943	Hptm. Frank	1
23.09.1943	Obltn. Schön	1
18.10.1943	Hptm. Meurer	1
22.10.1943	Hptm. Meurer	1
03.11.1943	Hptm. Meurer	1
21.01.1944	Hptm. Meurer	2
24.03.1944	Obltn. Nabrich	1
30.03.1944	Hptm. Modrow	2
11.04.1944	Obltn. Baake	1
11.04.1944	Fw. Rauer	1
22.04.1944	Hptm. Modrow	3
22.04.1944	Major Karlewski	1
22.04.1944	Uffz. Wildhagen	1
24.04.1944	Obltn. Baake	2
24.04.1944	Hptm. Modrow	2
26.04.1944	Ofw. Ströhlein	1
27.04.1944	Obltn. Hendeler	2
27.04.1944	Ltn. Hittler	1
01.05.1944	Hptm. Modrow	1
06.05.1944	Obltn. Baake	1 (Mosquito)
10.05.1944	Hptm. Strüning	1
10.05.1944	Obltn. Nabrich	1
11.05.1944	Hptm. Modrow	2
11.05.1944	Obltn. Baake	1
12.05.1944	Hptm. Modrow	2
12.05.1944	Obltn. Nabrich	1
12.05.1944	Hptm. Strüning	1
21.05.1944	Hptm. Strüning	1
21.05.1944	Obltn. Henseler	1
21.05.1944	Hptm. Modrow	1
21.05.1944	Hptm. Förster	1
21.05.1944	Major Karlewski	1
22.05.1944	Hptm. Strüning	1
22.05.1944	Obltn. Henseler	1
22.05.1944	Hptm. Modrow	1
22.05.1944	Major Karlewski	1
22.05.1944	Obltn. Baake	1
24.05.1944	Major Karlewski	1
24.05.1944	Hptm. Strüning	2
24.05.1944	Obltn. Nabrich	2
24.05.1944	Obltn. Henseler	1
27.05.1944	Fw. Morlock	1
27.05.1944	Fw. Rauer	1 (Mosquito)
28.05.1944	Hptm. Modrow	3
28.05.1944	Fw. Rauer	1 (Mosquito)
28.05.1944	Fw. Morlock	1
31.05.1944	Fw. Morlock	2
03.06.1944	Hptm. Strüning	1
03.06.1944	Ltn. Hittler	1
06.06.1944	Hptm. Strüning	1
11.06.1944	Hptm. Modrow	1 (Mosquito)
11.06.1944	Obltn. Nabrich	1 (Mosquito)
12.06.1944	(Obltn. Nabrich	1 (Mosquito)
13.06.1944	Hptm. Modrow	3
13.06.1944	Ltn. Hittler	1
16.06.1944	Obltn. Nabrich	2
16.06.1944	Hptm. Strüning	2
16.06.1944	Fw. Morlock	2
16.06.1944	Hptm. Förster	1
16.06.1944	Oppermann	1
16.06.1944	Bane	1
16.06.1944	Major Schäfer	1
16.06.1944	-	
18.06.1944	Hptm. Strüning	1 (Mosquito)
21.06.1944	Hptm. Strüning	4
02.07.1944	Olt Finke	1 (Mosquito)
06.07.1944	OFw. Stroelein	1
10.07.1944	Major Karlewski	1 (Mosquito)
18.07.1944	Hptm. Strüning	1 (Mosquito)
19.07.1944	Hptm. Strüning	1 (Mosquito)
21.07.1944	Hptm. Modrow	1
24.07.1944	Fw. Morlock	1
29.07.1944	Major Karlewski	1
29.07.1944	Major Schäfer	1
29.07.1944	Lt. Frieß	1
13.08.1944	Obtln. Nabrich	1
13.08.1944	Uffz. Frankenhauser	1
23.09.1944	Obltn. Schön	1
09.10.1944	Fw. Morlock	1
02.11.1944	Olt. Thurner	1
03.11.1944	OFw. Morlock	6 (+ 1 unknown)

Another photograph of G9+CL at the Royal Aeronautical Establishment (RAE) in England.

Captured He 219 A, Werknummer 190176. Photo: USAF

Apart from NJG 1, NJGr 10 in Werneuchen had several He 219s in addition to Bf 110 Gs, Fw 190 As and Bf 109 Gs. I/NJG 2 also had several Heinkel night fighters. Among others, this unit received six He 219s between May 3rd and 14th, 1944 (according to report by the "Technical Field Service" dated June 12, 1944).

Fifty-four He 219s were captured by Allied forces, including eight machines in Denmark. Three aircraft (T9-612 to 614) were taken to the USA and four (AM 20, 21, 43 and 44) to England. The Soviets handed over two captured machines to the Czechoslovakian Air Force in 1946. Except for one still unrestored He 219 in the USA (NASM, Silver Hill), all of the aircraft were scrapped.

The authors wish to express their gratitude to Herr Karl-Ernst Heinkel and his coworkers for their tremendous support. Our heartfelt thanks also go to all those who provided photographs.

Aircraft of 1./NJG 1 at Westerland airfield, Sylt in July 1945. The aircrafts' propellers were removed immediately at war's end. Photo: Petrick Collection

UHUs in Action

Four more photos of the He 219 V 1 taken during factory trials at Marienehe. Photo: M. Griehl

He 219 at Heinkel's Oranienburg factory. Photo: M. Griehl

He 219 Werknummer 290068 photographed during its delivery flight to NJG 1. Photo: M. Griehl

An He 219 photographed in service with NJG 1. Photo: M. Griehl

DV+DI, one of the three He 219 prototypes used for ejector seat trials at Rechlin in 1943/44.

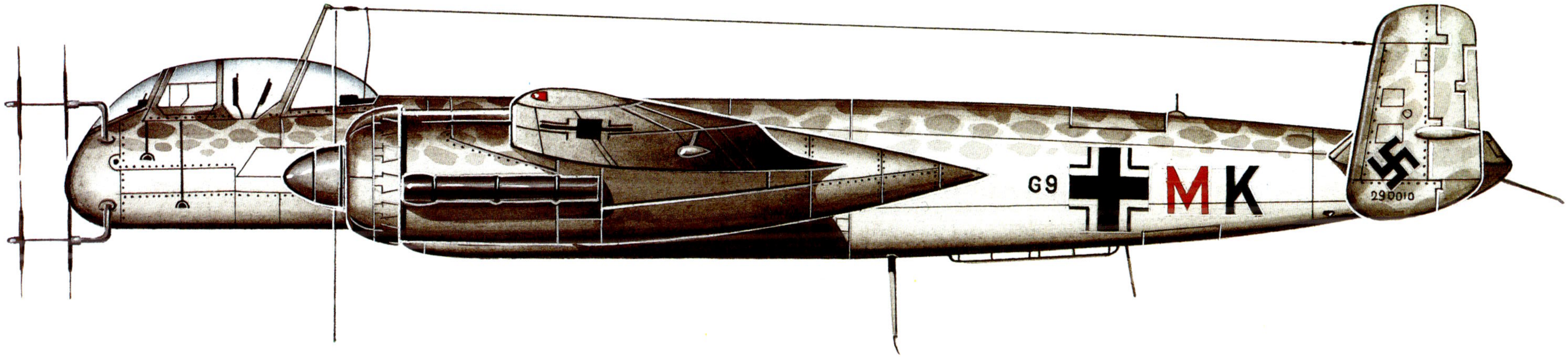

He 219 a-2 of 2./NJG 1. This aircraft was shot down by an RAF Tempest over Rechenfeld, Westphalia on November 29, 1944. The aircraft's pilot, Leutnant Fischer, was killed.

He 219 of 1/NJG 1 with black-painted undersides, aircraft found at Westerland, Sylt in 1945.

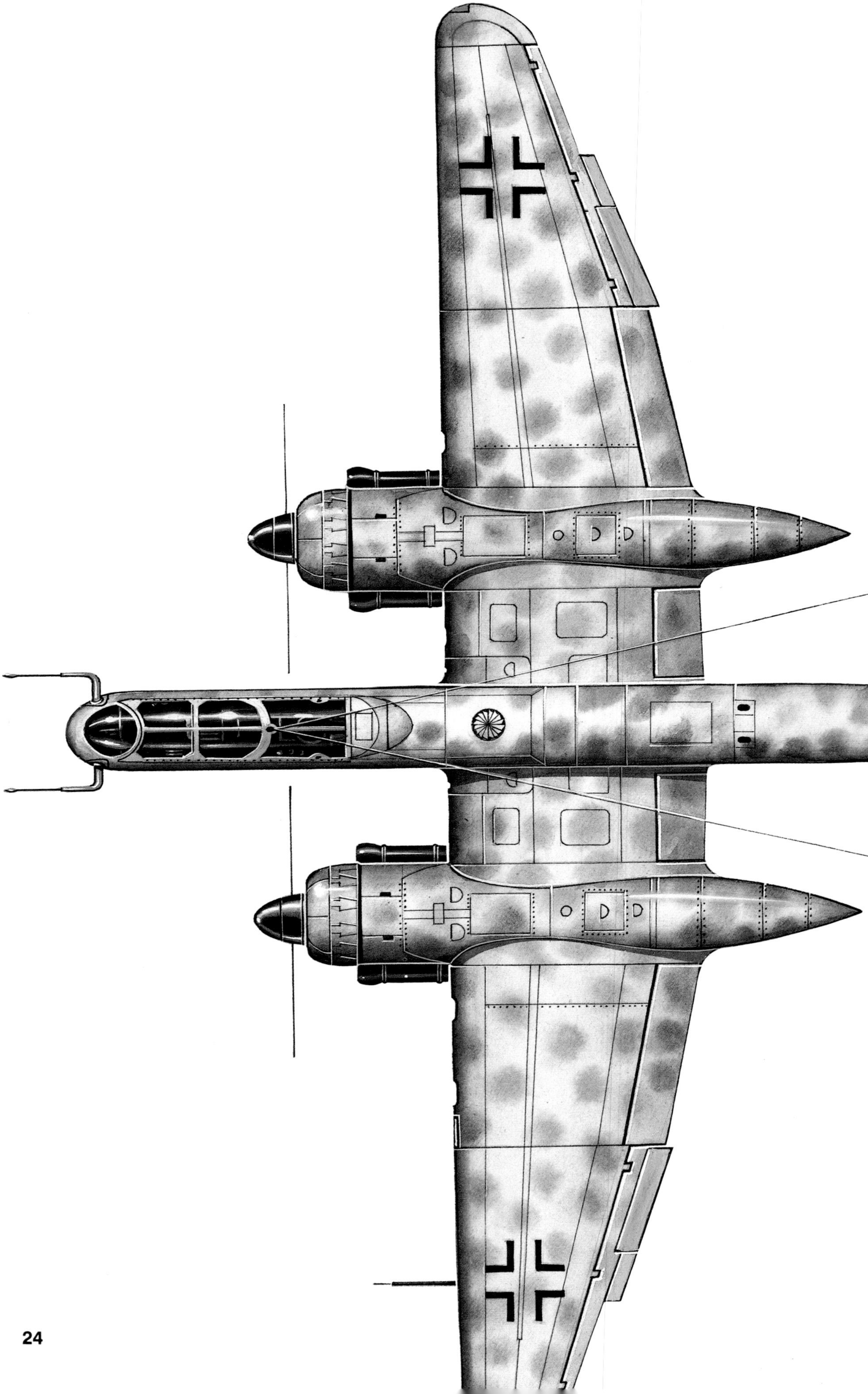

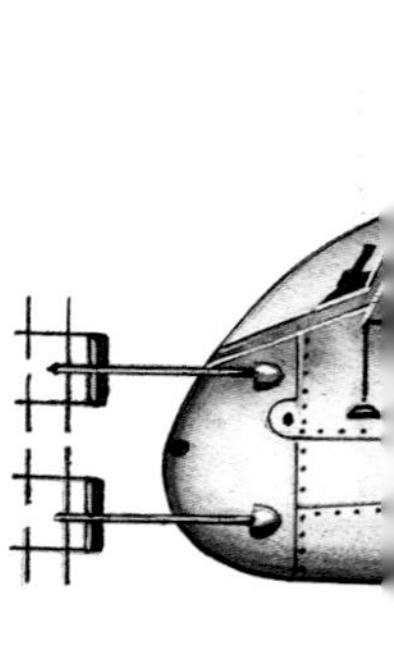

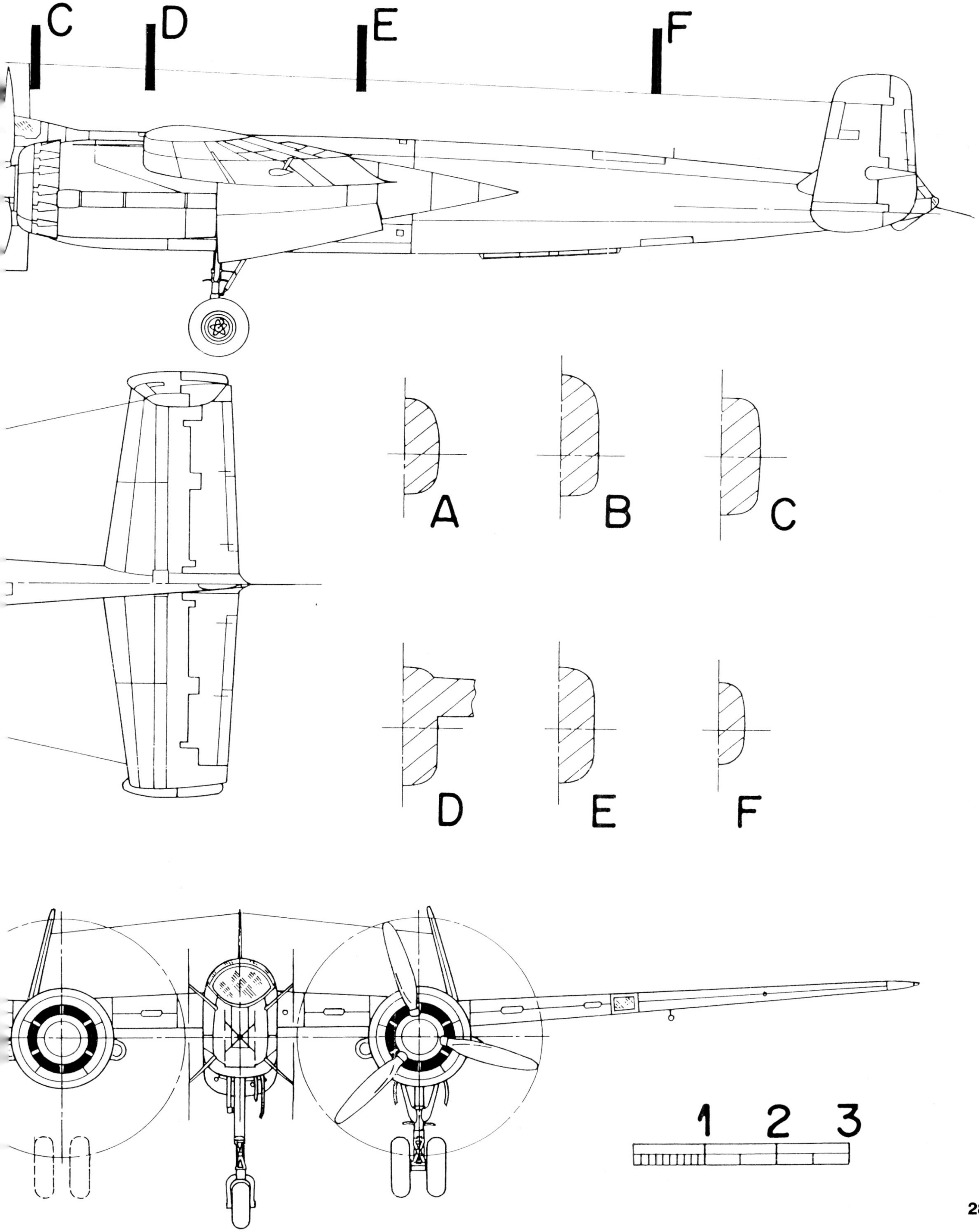
C
D
E
F
A
B
C
D
E
F
1
2
3

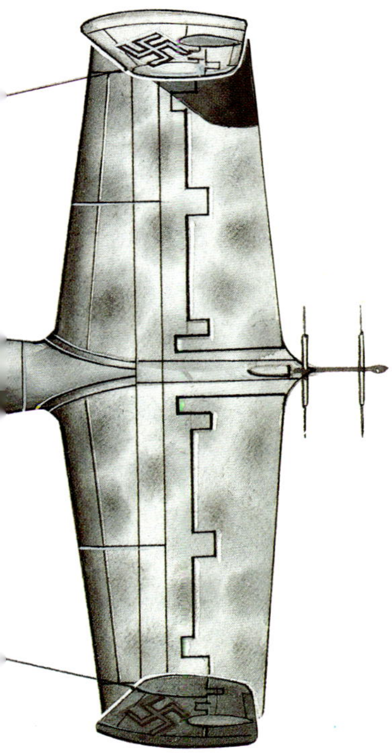

He 219 of 1/NJG 1 in standard finish.

Drawings by Ralf Swoboda

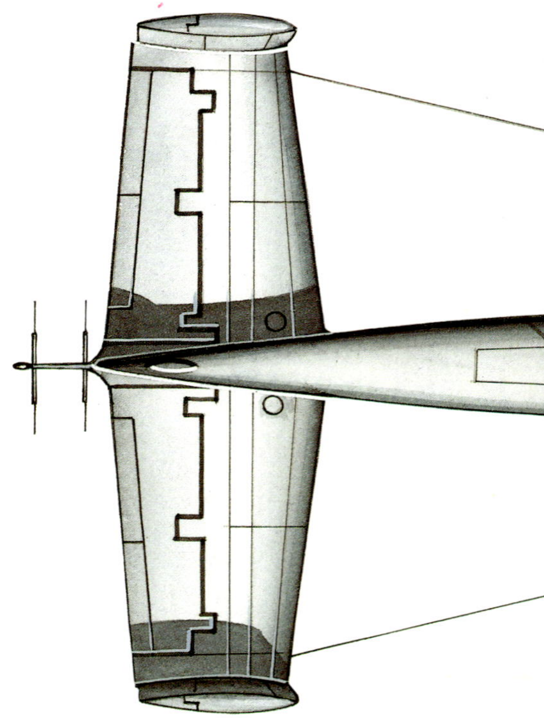

He 219 A-0 (FuG Lichtenstein 202) flown by Major Werner Streib.

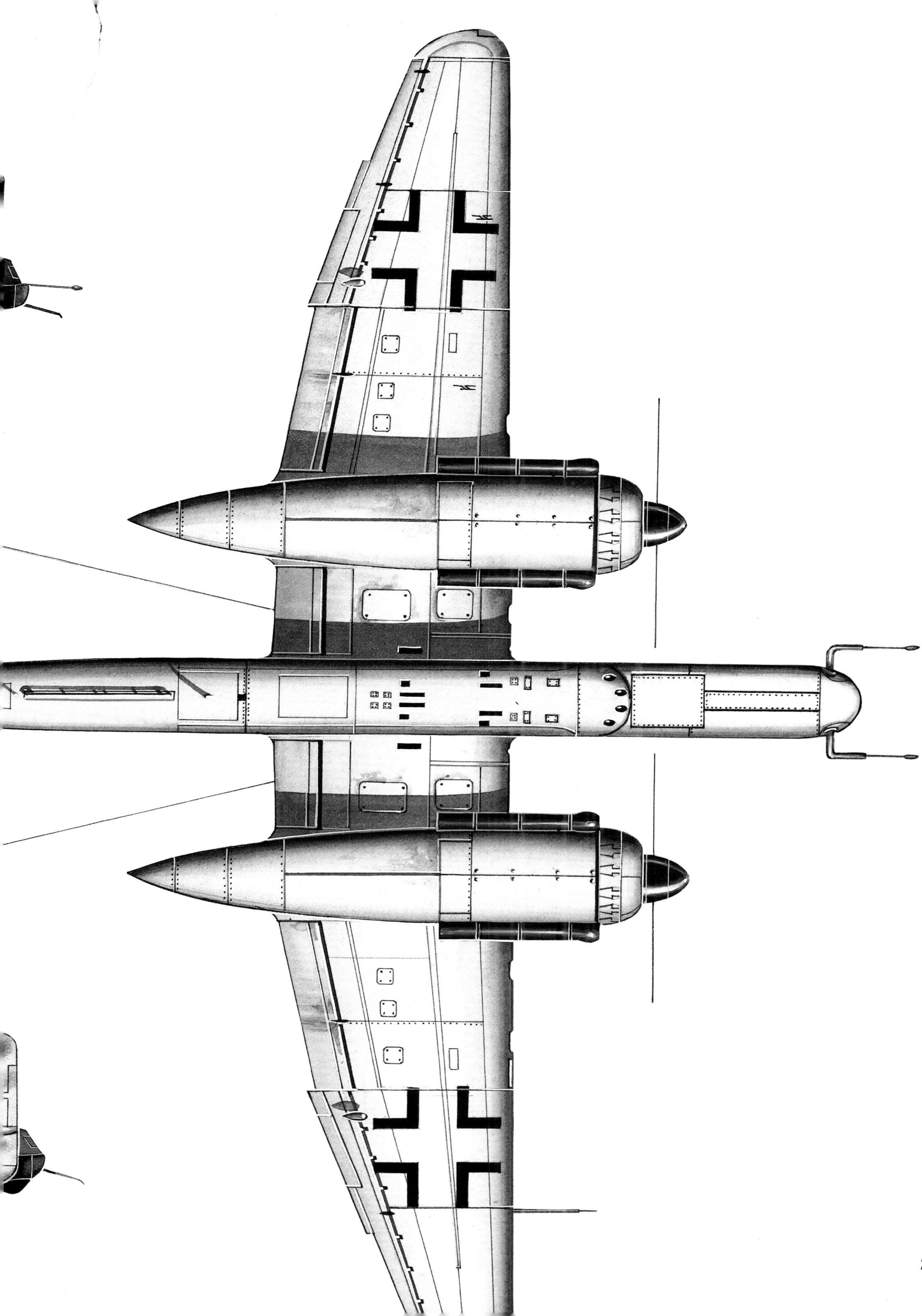

General arrangement drawing He 219. Drawing: Sh. Sinekal

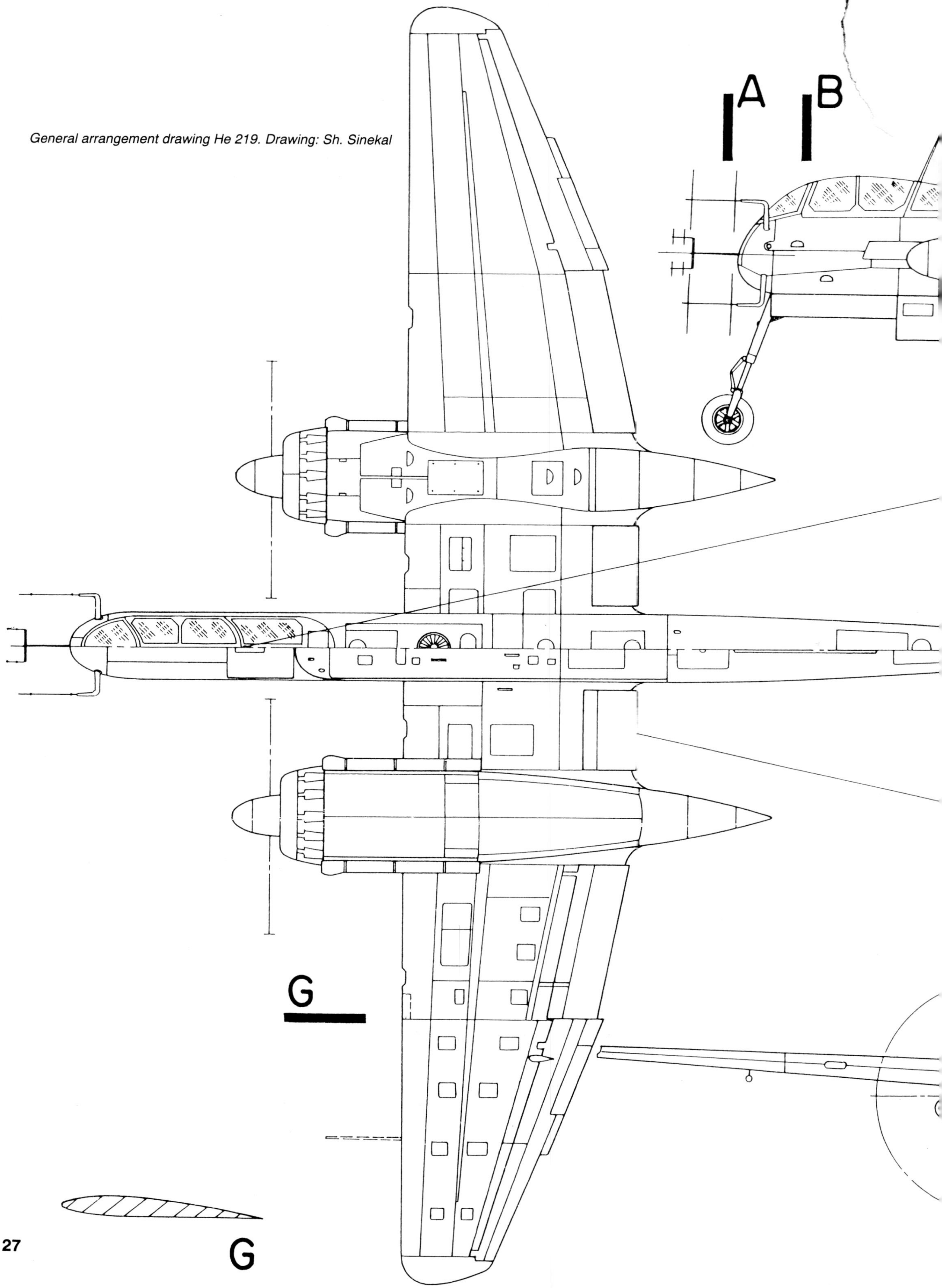

UHU Details

Front cockpit - side consoles

Reflector gunsight

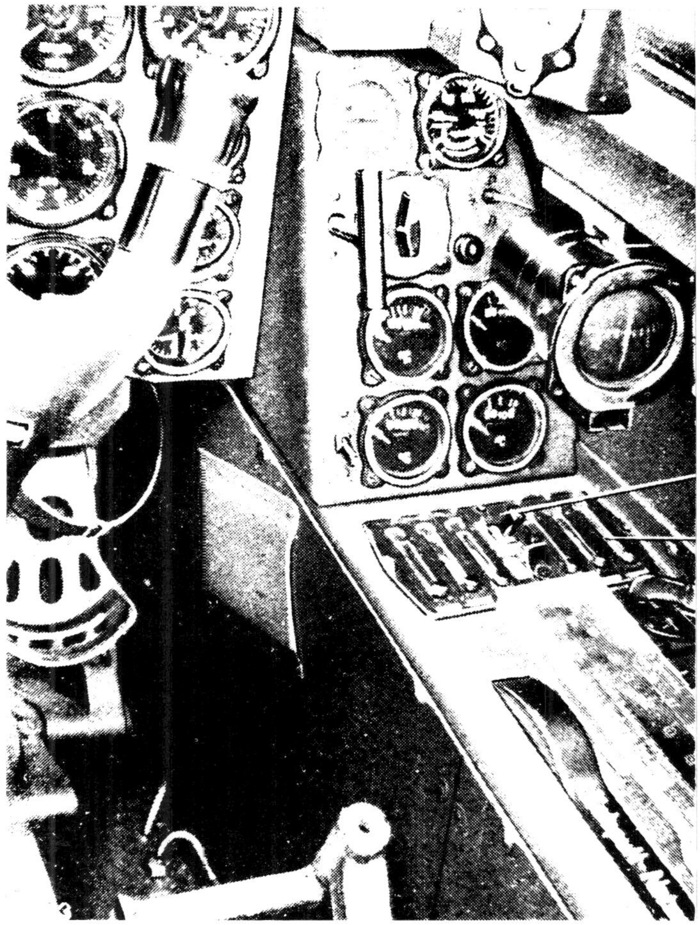

Right side console

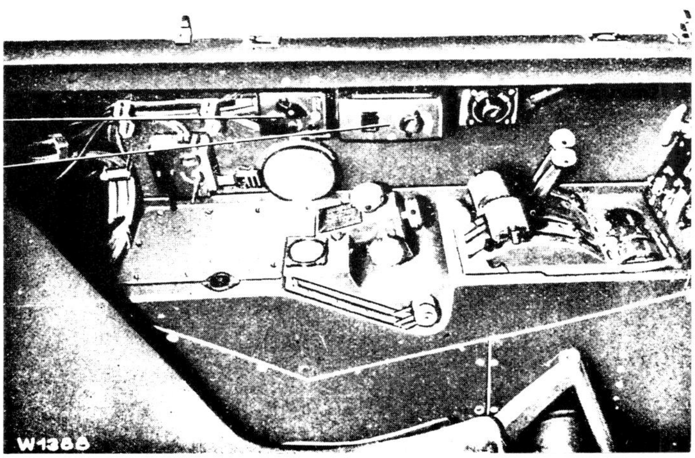

Left side console, forward section

Right side console, rear section

Rear cockpit

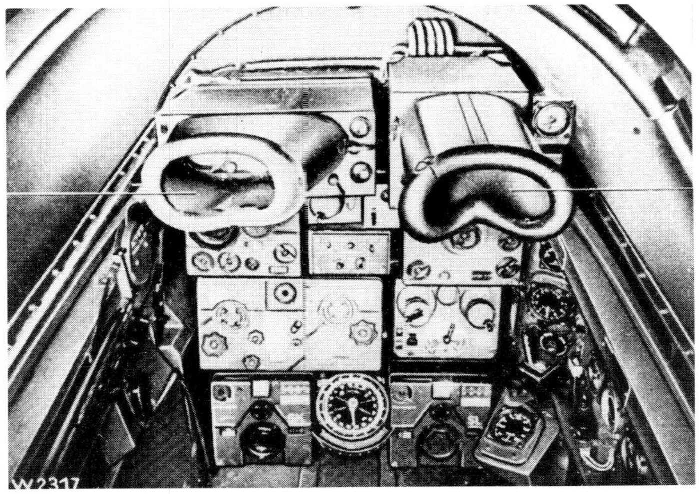

The same cockpit with radar scopes installed.

Rear cockpit with radar scopes removed.

Rear right side console.

Landing gear details

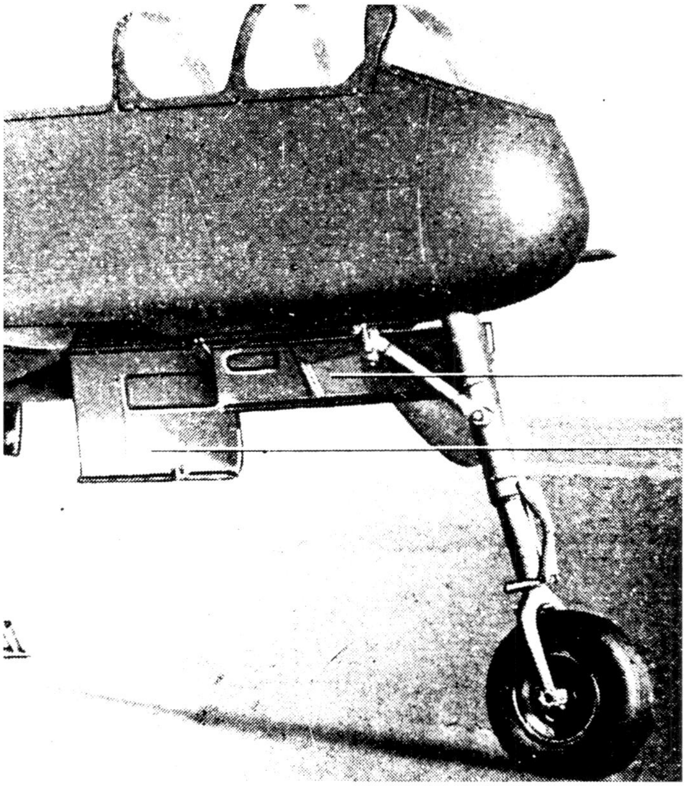

Factory photo of the nosewheel undercarriage member.

Front view of main undercarriage member.

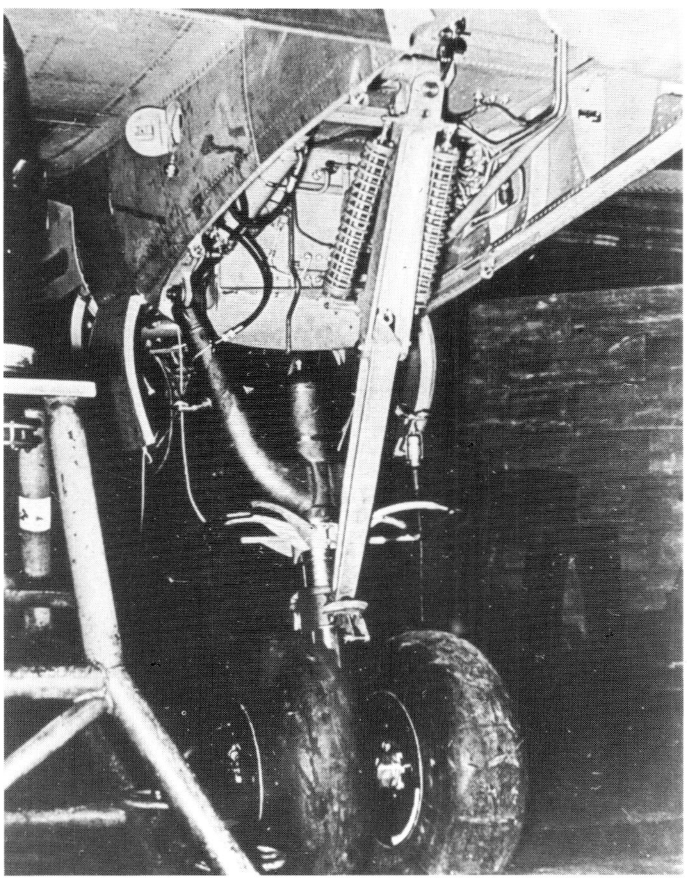

Rear view of main undercarriage member.

Detail photo of main undercarriage retraction mechanism.

Wing root armament access panels in the open position.

Detail shot of radiator flaps.

UHU Wrecks

G9+DH, Werknummer 290004, an He 219 of 1/NJG 1. It is not known where this photograph was taken. Photo: M. Griehl

Front view of G9+DH. Note the spiral pattern on the aircraft's starboard spinner. Photo: M. Griehl

Side view of G9+DH. The entire forward section of the aircraft appears to be painted in a darker camouflage scheme. The dark finish in the area of the exhaust is interesting. Photo: M. Griehl

G9+VH of 1/NJG 1, photographed at Westerland, Sylt in 1945. Photo: M. Griehl

Tying down and covering the aircraft.

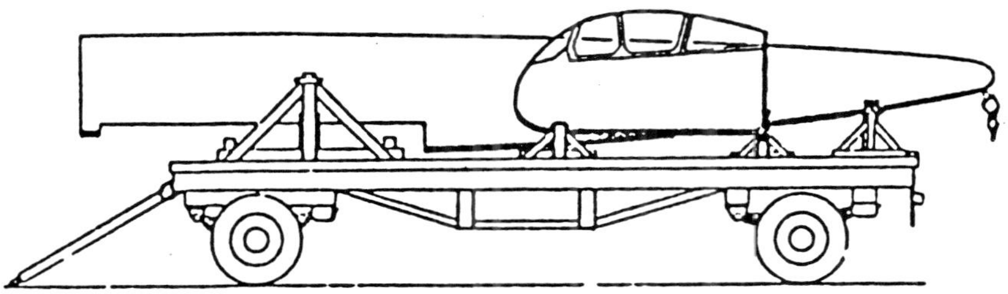

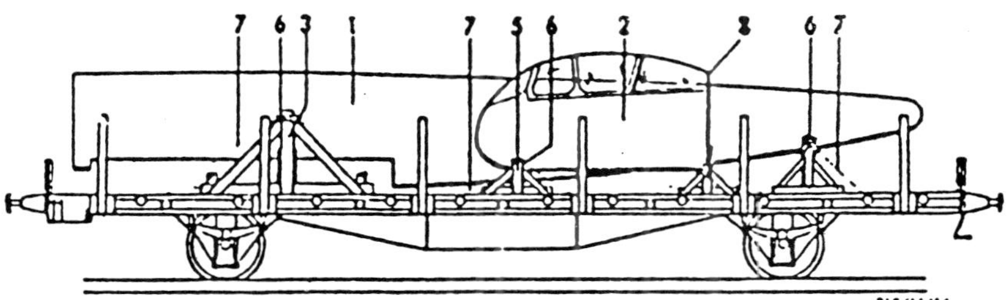

1	Fuselage
2	Cockpit
3	Middle loading jack
5	Forward loading jack
6	Tie-down fittings
7	Tie-down rope
8	Loading jack for cockpit at Frame 9

Illustration 8: Fuselage on S-Car

CONTENTS

Brief description of the He 219

TYPENBLATT He219

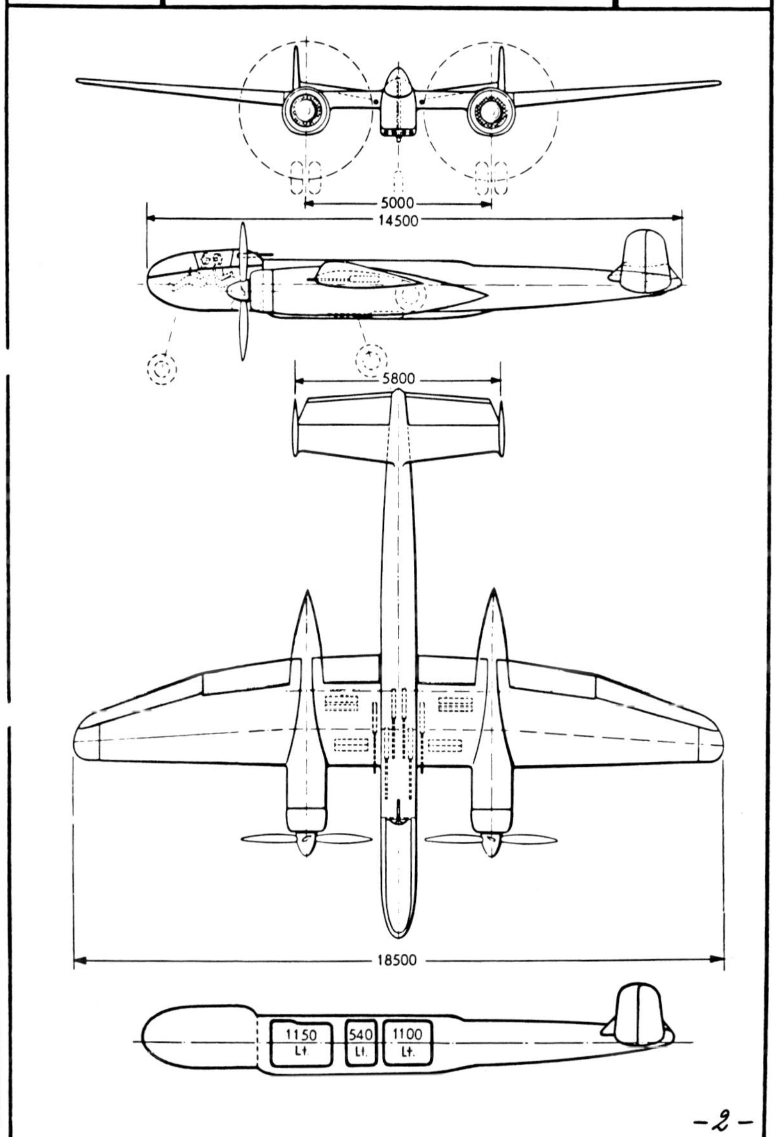

Geheim

-2-

Kurzbeschreibung He 219 F. Gr. Nr. 8001/5 An/Ki Dez. 1942.

RÜSTSATZ I He219

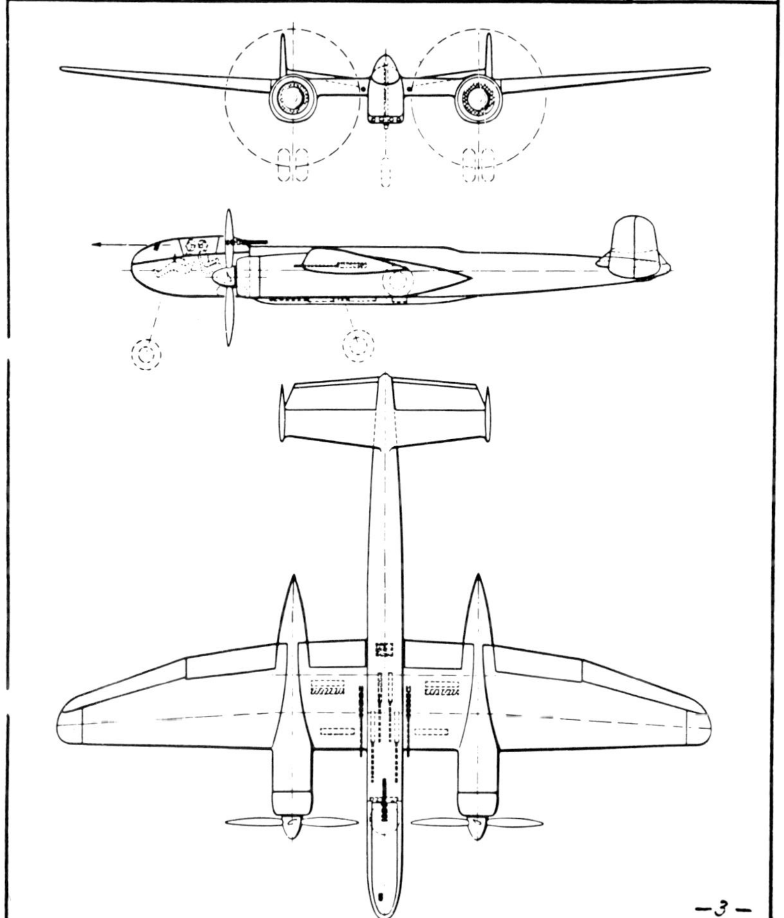

-3-

Waffeneinbau:	2 Flügelwaffen	Mg 151/20	Vo:	705 m/s
(Starre Schußwaffen)	2 Rumpfw. vorn	Mg 151/20	Treffermöglichkeiten:	72 Schuß/s
	2 „ hinten	Mg 151/20	Feuerdauer gesamt:	25 sec
Munition:	je 300 Schuß		Schaltzentrale:	
	je 300 „		Revi 16 B:	
	je 300 „		Bewegliche Schußwaffe	1 Mg 131 (handgerichtet)
			Munition	500 Schuß

Geheim

Kurzbeschreibung He 219 F. Gr. Nr. 8001 7 An/Ki Dez. 1942.

RÜSTSATZ III — He219

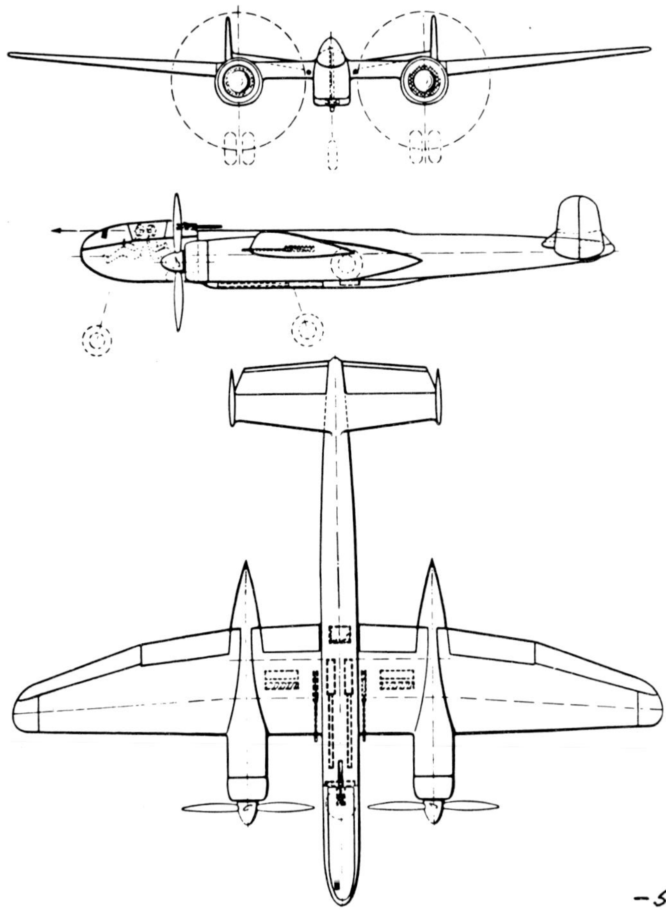

–5–

Waffeneinbau:	2 Flügelwaffen	Mg 151/20
(Starre Schußwaffen)	2 Rumpfw.	2 Mk 103
Munition:	je 300 Schuß 20 mm	
	je 100 „ 30 mm	

	Mg 151/20	Mk 103
Vo:	705 m/s	720 m/s
Treffermöglichkeiten:	24 Schuß/s	14 Schuß/s
Gesamt:	38 Schuß/s	
Feuerdauer gesamt:	25 s	14 s
Schaltzentrale:		
Revi 16 B:		
Bewegliche Schußwaffe	1 Mg 131 (handgerichtet)	
Munition	500 Schuß	

Geheim

Kurzbeschreibung He 219 F. Gr. Nr. 8001 9 An/Ki Dez. 1942.

RÜSTSATZ II — He219

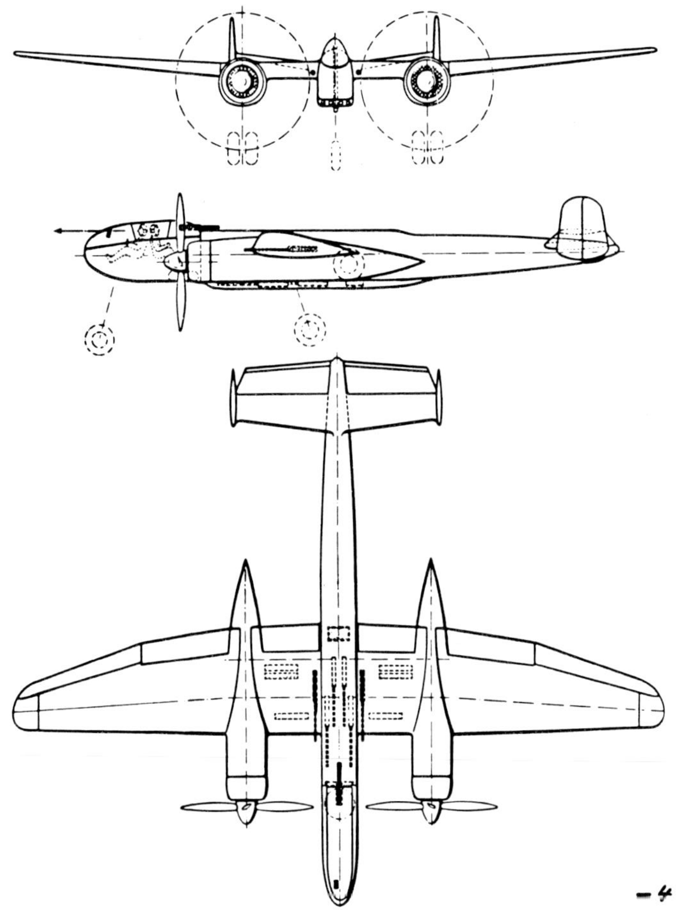

–4–

Waffeneinbau:	2 Flügelwaffen	Mg 151/20
(Starre Schußwaffen)	2 Rumpfw. vorn	Mk 108
	2 „ hinten	Mk 108
Munition:	je 300 Schuß 20 mm	
	je 100 „ 30 mm	
	je 100 „ 30 mm	

	Mg 151/20	Mk 108
Vo:	705 m/s	540 m/s
Treffermöglichkeiten:	24 Schuß/s	40 Schuß/s
Feuerdauer gesamt:	25 s	10 s
Schaltzentrale:		
Revi 16 B:		
Bewegliche Schußwaffe	1 Mg 131 (handgerichtet)	
Munition	500 Schuß	

Geheim

Kurzbeschreibung He 219 F. Gr. Nr. 8001 8 An/Ki Dez. 1942.

TRENNSTELLEN **He219**

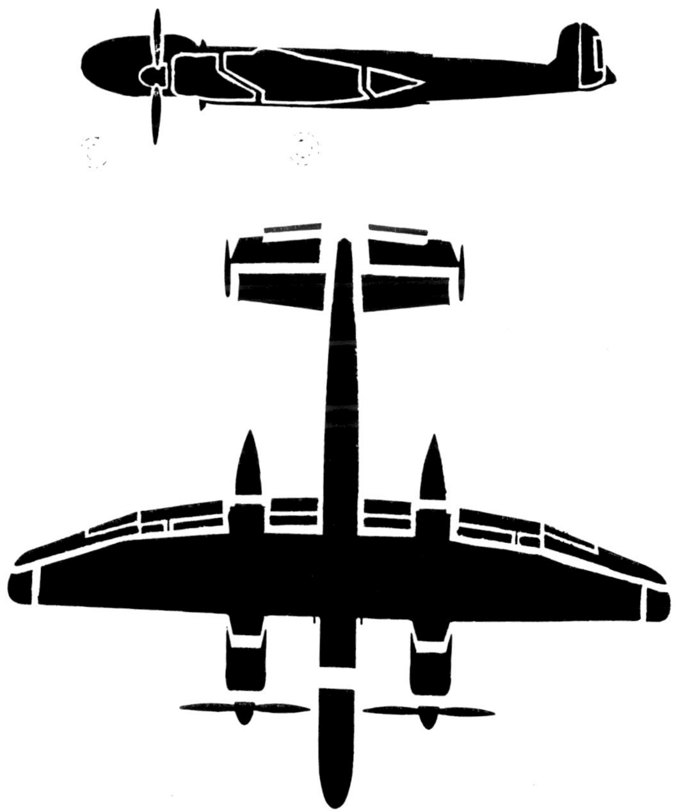

—6—

Flight Test Results **He 219**

I. As of 9.12.42, 16 flights have been carried out with the He 219 V 1 totalling 7 hours 6 minutes.

II. Performance flights could not be carried out on account of weather.

III. Rough estimates have revealed that the radiators are adequate for tropical use. The engines have given no cause for complaint.

Assessment of Handling Qualities by EHF:

1. The maximum speed achieved to date is 500 kph. Higher speeds were not attained because of the appearance of mild vibration in the ailerons, which must first be eliminated.
2. Directional stability at high speeds is so great that loss of control is impossible, but also great that corrections cannot be made during takeoff. It is therefore important that the aircraft is placed precisely in the direction of takeoff.
3. The landing is simple. The nosewheel prevents bouncing on touchdown, even if the landing does not take place at CCmax.
4. The uncomfortable nosewheel effect, the rapid increase in the angle of attack on liftoff, is not evident.
5. The control forces are not yet completely harmonized, however in general they are acceptable in the neutral position, still too great at large deflections.Control effectiveness is good and adequate for all flight regimes and in all CG positions.
6. Stability about the roll axis is still just adequate even in the most aft CG position. Damping has not yet been adequately investigated.
7. Static stability about the vertical axis is too weak. The vertical stabilizers were enlarged after the last flight. Results not yet available.
8. The rolling moment is sufficiently present as with the He 177. It remains to be determined whether the rolling moment is still sufficient with greater static stability about the vertical axis.
9. Severe pitch changes occur on retracting the landing flaps, as with the He 177. These are reduced by changing the angle of incidence of the horizontal stabilizer.
10. Pitch changes during undercarriage retraction are very minor.
11. Pitch changes about the vertical axis occur when engine power settings are changed; these are attributable to the inadequate stability about the vertical axis.

Summary:

In summary it can be said that the aircraft is certainly not yet fully developed, but it is capable of being flown by any average pilot.

Geheim

Geheim!

GESCHWINDIGKEITEN — He 219

F = 44,5 m²; b = 18,5 m; Λ = 7,7
Motor: **DB 603 A** (i = 1,93)
Schraube: D = 3,6 m; Z = 4; t/D = 0,08

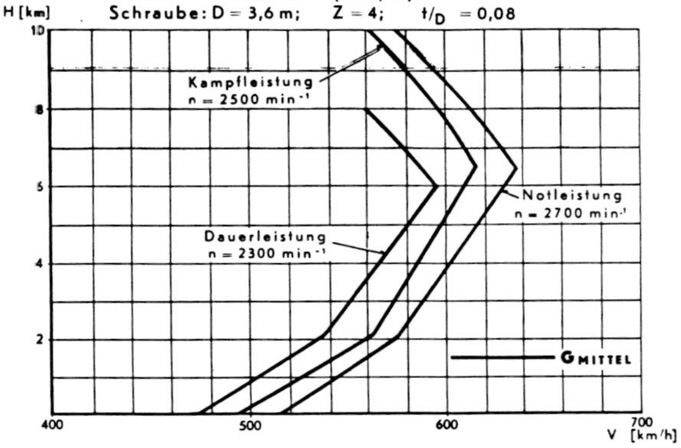

F = 44,5 m²; b = 18,5 m; Λ = 7,7
Motor: **DB 603 G** (i = 1,93)
Schraube: D = 3,6 m; Z = 4; t/D = 0,08

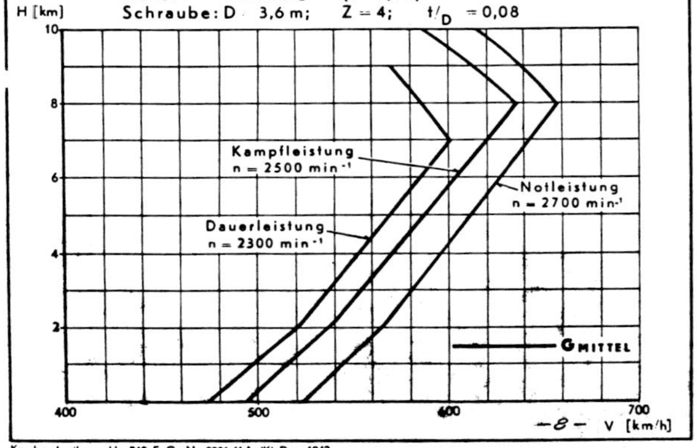

Geheim

Kurzbeschreibung He 219 F. Gr. Nr. 8001-11 An/Ki Dez. 1942.

STEIGGESCHWINDIGKEITEN UND STEIGZEITEN — He 219

Motor: 2 × **DB 603 A** F = 44,5 m²; b = 18,5 m; Λ = 7,7
Schraube: D = 3,6 m; Z·t/D = 0,32; (i = 1,93)

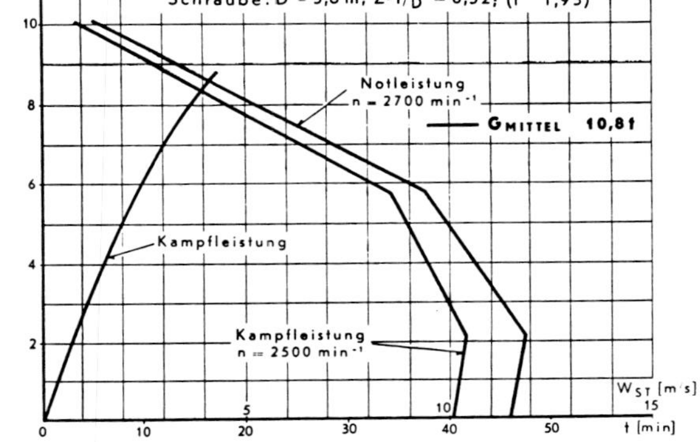

Motor: 2 × **DB 603 G** F = 44,5 m²; b = 18,5 m; Λ = 7,7
Schraube: D = 3,6 m; Z·t/D = 0,32; (i = 1,93)

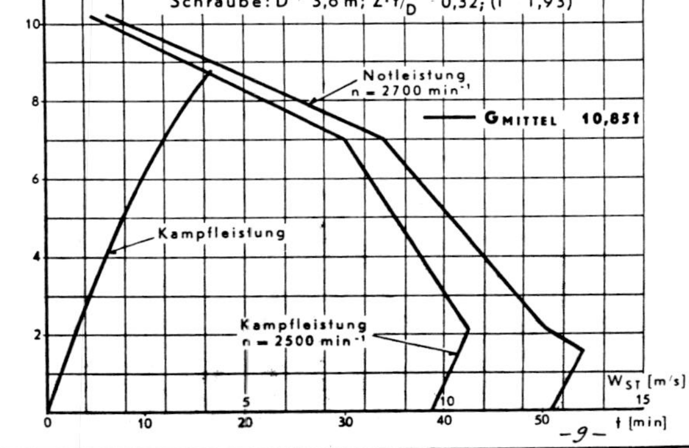

Geheim

Kurzbeschreibung He 219 F. Gr. Nr. 8001 12An/Ki Dez. 1942.

GIPFELHÖHE IM EINMOTORENFLUG — He 219

F = 44,5 m²; b = 18,5 m; Λ = 7,7
Motor: **DB 603 A** (i = 1,93)

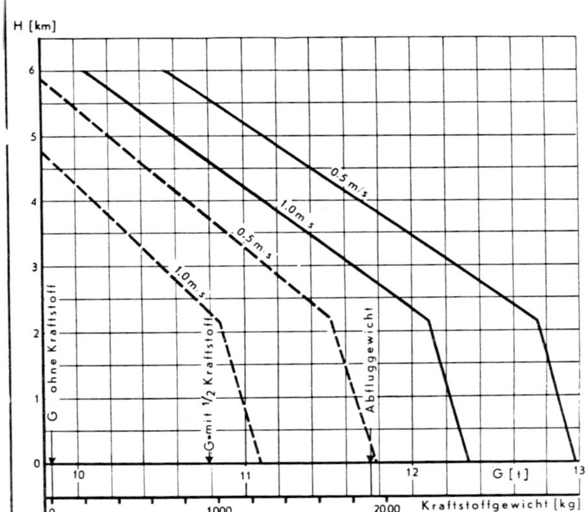

——— **Kampfleistung** n = 2500 U/min; p_L = 1,3 ata

– – – – **max. Dauerleistung** n = 2300 U/min; p_L = 1,2 ata

Geheim

Kurzbeschreibung He 219 F. Gr. Nr. 8001 13An/Ki Dez. 1942.

ROLLWEG UND WEG BIS 20 m HÖHE — He 219

F = 44,5 m²; b = 18,5 m; Λ = 7,7
Motor: 2 × **DB 603 A**

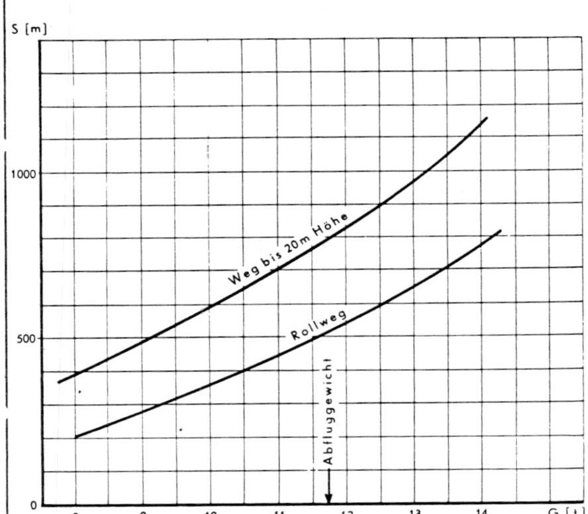

Bodenreibung μ = 00,3

15°C, 760 m/m QS; 0 m/s Wind

Geheim

Kurzbeschreibung He 219 F. Gr. Nr. 8001/14An/Ki Dez. 1942.

HEINKEL	Specification Sheet	He 219

Wingspan Wing Area Wing Loading at 11.75 tons Weight to Power Ratio at 11.75 tons				18.5 m² 44.5 m² 264 kg/m 3.36 kg H.P.
Engines: 2 x DB 603 A, gearing 1.93 Takeoff power at 2,700 rpm Climb and combat power at 2,500 rpm at sea level Climb and combat power at 2,500 rpm at 5.7 km				 2 x 1750 H.P. 2 x 1580 H.P. 2 x 1510 H.P.
Metal propellers, VDM type. Diameter				3.6 m
Armament: Fixed forward firing weapons (20mm) Dorsal position, hand operated				 6 x MG 151 MG 131
Structural Strength: safety limit 6 G at weight of 12.2 tons				
Basic Weight Crew Fuel (2590 l, .74 kg/l) Oil Ammunition **Takeoff Weight**				9030 kg 200 kg 1930 kg 142 kg 484 kg 11750 kg
Maximum Speed at combat power, 1/2 fuel	H.P. 3160 3000		Height (km) 0 6.5	 490 kph 615 kph
Average cruising speed and calculated range *) (without gliding flight)	2750 2760 1800	g/PSh 215 215 215	 0 0 6	 470 kph - 1415 km 595 kph - 1720 km 485 kph - 2240 km
Time to climb at takeoff weight to			2 4 6 8	3.5 min 7.2 min 11.5 min 18 min
Service Ceiling, 2 engines after takeoff " " " 1/2 fuel				9900 m 10300 m
Single-engine Flight: Weight at 1 m/sec at combat power Climb speed at height of 2 km at max. sustained power				 12100 kg 10850 kg
Takeoff roll and distance to height of 20 m Climb speed at liftoff Landing speed, weight = 10.4 tons				520/780 m 3.9 m/sec 150 kph

*) Allowances made for run-up, takeoff, climb and 2% reserve.

—12—

Geheim

Kurzbeschreibung He 219 F. Gr. 8001 / 4 Dezember 1942

This document describes the firing of an ejector seat from an He 219. For security reasons the aircraft was described as an He 111.

Copy KOL/-He.

Heinkel Rostock to
Heinkel Vienna

31.5.44 14.30 hours FS No. 21722

Priority!!!

To Prof. Dr. Heinkel, Dir. Francke, Mr. Schwärzler, Mr. Hilber.

Subject: Accident He 111 N Werk-Nr. 190116

During the night of May 19th-20th Leutnant Fries, Technical Officer of the 2nd Gruppe in Deelen, was in action with the above Werk-Nr. The right engine caught fire as a result of enemy fire at a height of 7000 meters, as reported by TAD crew ejected. Pilot suffered minor concussion and 2 cuts on the forehead. The radio operator, Feldwebel Staffer, suffered a fracture of the skull base. Both members of the crew were visited by Mr. Maciejewski, TAD, in hospital in Herzogenbusch, Holland.

Leutnant Fried stated that he did not intend to bail out, rather that he only intended to jettison the canopy for safety reasons. At the same moment he activated the cockpit canopy emergency release he felt a blow on the head and lost consciousness. When he came to again the radio operator had already left the aircraft. The aircraft was at a height of approximately 2500 m. Blinded by the heavy flow of blood from the two cuts on his forehead, he was forced to decide to bail out although the aircraft was still flyable and the fire in the engine, which had previously been shut down, was almost extinguished. He activated the ejector system, during ejection he inclined his head forward, resulting in a mild muscle sprain in his neck. The radio operator's injuries resulted from landing on the roof of a house. The aircraft was a total loss.

signed Thesenfitz, Technical Field Service

B. Additional Publications

Engine handbook for the Mercedes-Benz DB 603 A aero engine.
Brief operating instructions for the VDM variable-pitch propeller on the DB 603 A.

Works publication	1003. On-board heating equipment.
D. (Luft) T.3870	Starting of Aero Engines in Winter. September 1942 edition.
D. (Luft) T.8002	Description and Instructions for Use of the Servicing Kit for Plexiglass.
D. (Luft) T.5303	Engine Pumps for Hydraulic Systems.
D. (Luft) T.4062	
D. (Luft) T.4601	Emergency Landing in Enemy Territory.
L.Dv.72/1	
D. (Luft) T.3370/21	Cold Start Chart (inclosed in Bv.Fl.)

Brief Description of the Aircraft

A. General

Cantilever, twin-engined, all-metal, mid-wing monoplane with 2 propellers, projecting forward fuselage (full-view cockpit), tapered rear fuselage, high-mounted twin vertical stabilizers, trapezoid-shaped horizontal stabilizer, medium wingspan, slim airfoil section, one-piece trapezoidal wing with rounded tips, normal forward-positioned engines (clockwise rotation), two-part main undercarriage retracting rearward into the engine nacelles and a rearward-retracting nosewheel.

B. Significant Design Features

1. Fuselage

All-metal design (monocoque construction). Rectangular cross section with sharply rounded corners, tapered to the rear. Fuselage is divided into cockpit, forward fuselage, rear fuselage and tail.

The cockpit is bolted to the forward fuselage. Forward fuselage, rear fuselage and tail are riveted together. Three fuel tanks are housed in the forward fuselage. Cockpit and fuel tank areas are separated by bulkhead ribs. (Fuselage walls are parallel in this area.) Cockpit is partially armored with glazed hood. Located on the fuselage side walls left and right is a circuit conduit, with good accessibility from outside by means of access panels.

2. Wing Assembly

Cantilever, one-piece wing with main and end spars and removable end caps on the wingtips.

The engine nacelles form part of the wing, their monocoque bodies also serve as engine bearers. The undercarriage attachment points are located on the main and end spars symmetrical to the center of the engine nacelles. There is an oil tank (105 l) and a reservoir for propeller de-icing fluid located in each wing in the area of the engine nacelles between the main and rear spars and between Ribs 2 and 3. The reservoir (17 l) for the hydraulic system is installed on the roof of the left undercarriage bay. Slotted flaps and ailerons occupy the entire trailing edge of the wing. The wing leading edges are equipped with a warm-air de-icing system.

3. Empennage

The horizontal stabilizer is a cantilever, one-piece structure. The stabilizer profile is asymmetric. The stabilizer leading edge is protected against icing by warm air (Kärcher heater).

The vertical stabilizer consists of tail fins which are installed as outboard fins on the horizontal stabilizer. The shape of the vertical stabilizer is trapezoidal with sharply rounded corners.

Ailerons and landing flaps are designed as slotted ailerons and slotted flaps respectively. The ailerons are coupled with the landing flaps. The horizontal and vertical stabilizers are each equipped with a trim tab, which in the case of the elevator also serves as a balancing tab. A trim tab is installed on the left aileron. The trim tabs are adjustable from the pilot's position in the cockpit. All control surfaces and trim tabs are 100% balanced.

4. Undercarriage

Two-part main undercarriage with four mainwheels, retract rearward into the engine nacelles hydraulically and a rearward-retracting nosewheel. In the retracted position the nosewheel lies beneath the cockpit floor. Extension of the main undercarriage and nosewheel is hydraulic.

Emergency extension: by weight of undercarriage after mechanical release by means of emergency lever, nosewheel by compressed air in an emergency.

5. Flight Controls

The flight controls consist of elevator, rudder and aileron control, elevator, rudder and aileron trimming, landing flap settings, tailplane trimming and control locks.

Elevators activated by pulling and pushing, ailerons activated by turning the horn-type grip on the control column, rudders activated by movable foot pedals. Control inputs transmitted by control rods via bell cranks.

Elevator, rudder and aileron trimming by adjusting handwheels in the cockpit.

Hydraulic setting of landing flaps by switching on a pilot valve. Emergency operation of landing flaps by compressed air.

Tailplane trimming is automatic on setting landing flaps.

Elevators, rudders and ailerons may be locked in neutral position by pulling a lever in the cockpit.

Directional control is equipped with a K 12 autopilot.

6. Power Plants and Engine Systems

Two DB 603 liquid-cooled, twelve-cylinder, four-cycle, fuel-injected engines with gear reduction of 1.93 : 1.

Single-stage hydraulic supercharger for rated altitude of 5.8 km and automatic boost pressure control. Each engine drives a VDM metal variable-pitch propeller (three-bladed) with manual electro-mechanical adjustment.

The engines are designed as quick-change power plants.

Three protected fuel tanks in the fuselage. Delivery of fuel by the tank pumps to the fuel pumps through two systems of fuel cocks and two filters either from Tank 1 or Tanks 2 and 3 after selection from cockpit. Oil tank in each of the left and right engine nacelles.

Each propeller is served by a reservoir (20 l) for de-icing fluid located in the left and right engine nacelles.

The cooling system for each engine with radiator and so on is installed on the engine as a unit.

7. Hydraulic System

Two hydraulic fluid pumps, driven by the left and right engines.

A hydraulic fluid tank (17 l) in the left engine nacelle.

Hydraulically-activated are:

High-pressure system (to 90 kg/cm²)	wheel brakes undercarriage
Low-pressure system (30 kg/cm²)	landing flaps radiator flaps
Emergency activation includes:	lowering of nosewheel setting landing flaps

D. Maximum Allowable Speeds

Altitude meters	Airspeed kph
0	provisional maximum
3000	allowable speed = 700 kph
5000	
7000	

Flight with undercarriage extended .... 300 kph
Flight with landing flaps lowered (landing position) .... 300 kph
During extension and retraction of undercarriage .... 300 kph

E. Rate of Delivery

The rate of delivery is laid down in the L-File and is to be taken from this.

F. Fluids

Fuel .... B 4 (87 Octane)
Starter fuel .... aero starter fuel
Lubricating oil .... Red Ring
Coolant .... 48.5% water
.... 50% glycol
.... 1.5% preservative oil
De-icing fluid .... LEF 25 A
Hydraulic Fluid .... Aero Hydraulic Fluid

G. Tank and Reservoir Contents

1. Fuel

Tank 1 (forward) .... 1100 liters
Tank 2 (middle) .... 500 liters
Tank 3 (rear) .... 990 liters
....
Total contents .... 2590 liters

H. Performance and Consumptions

	Performance Type	Output Pressure H.P. +2.5%	Revolutions RPM +2%	Boost atm. +.02	Fuel Consumption l/hr
0	Takeoff and Emergency Power	1750	2700	1.40	565
0	Climb and Combat Power	1580	2500	1.30	475
0	Maximum Allowable Continuous Output	1375	2300	1.20	400
5.7	Emergency Power	1620	2700	1.40	535
5.7	Climb and Combat Power	1510	2500	1.30	465
5.4	Maximum Allowable Continuous Output	1400	2300	1.20	410
5.0	Maximum Economical Continuous Output	1170	2000	1.05	325

J. Ranges

Ranges are listed in the air route tables.

K. Operating Data

1. During Run-up

Propeller position .... 12 o'clock
Revolutions .... 2400 rpm
Boost pressure .... 1.30 atm.
Magneto test at .... 2000 rpm
Maximum drop 50 rpm, otherwise change sparkplugs
Fuel pressure .... 1.6-1.8 kg/cm³
Oil pressure .... 3-8 kg/cm³
Oil inlet temperature .... 20-80 deg C
Coolant outlet temperature .... 60-115 deg C

2. In Flight

Oil pressure .... 3 kg/cm³
Fuel pressure .... 1.6-1.8 kg/cm³
Oil inlet temperature at least .... 20 deg C
    short term maximum .... 85 deg C
Coolant outlet temperature normal .... 90-100 deg C
    short term maximum .... 115 deg C

2. Starter Fuel

2 x 4 liters. One tank on the rear side of the fire wall in the left and right undercarriage bays.

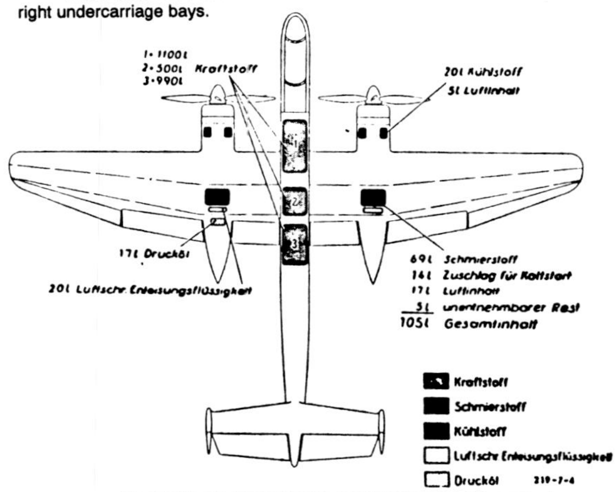

Illustration 7: Fluid Tanks and Reservoirs (Overview)

3. Lubricating Oil

2 x 105 liters. Total contents (maximum capacity 69 liters each), remaining space for cold start, air and foam forming.

4. Coolant

2 x 24 liters. Two reservoirs on the left and right sides of both the left and right engines. Total contents of the cooling system of an engine approximately 80 liters.

5. De-icing Fluid

2 x 20 liters. One reservoir in each engine nacelle in the space between the main and rear spars.

6. Hydraulic Fluid

17-liter reservoir (maximum capacity 11.7 liters) in the left engine nacelle on the roof of the undercarriage bay.

Zulassung PK + QA	Muster He 219 A-0	Werk-Nr. 1900
Verwendungs-gruppe H 4	Sturzflug V max. (Bahn)	700 km/h

Motorbelastungsgrenzen

Muster DB 603	Zul. Zeit	Lade-druck	Drehzahlen 0 - km	Drehzahlen üb. km
Start	1 Min.	1,40	2700	
Flug	30 Min.	1,30	2500	
	max. Dauer	1,20	2300	
Sturzflug	n max. = 2750 U/min			
Stand	Luftschr. 12°° n = ~ 2550			

Betriebstemperatur und Drücke

	Kühlstoff Austritt max.	Kühlstoff Höhe km	Schmierstoff Eintritt norm.	Schmierstoff Eintritt max.
Temp.	115 °	0—2,5	70-80 °	85 °
Druck	—		min. 3 kg/cm²	

Kraftstoffdruck: 1,6—1,8 kg/cm²

Betankungsanweisung

	Kraftstoff	Schmierstoff
Art	B 4	Rotring
Menge	2600 Ltr.	155 Ltr.

Reichweite bei Dauerleistung
für 2500 Ltr. Kraftstoffgesamtmenge

Flug-höhe km	Lade-druck	Dreh-zahl	Ver-brauch l/h	Wahre Geschw. km/h (Wind-stille)	Gesamtflug Zeit h'	Gesamtflug Strecke km (Wind-stille)
0	1,20	2300	885	450	2,70	*1200
2,1	1,20	2300	905	500	2,60	1300
6,0	1,20	2300	910	565	2,60	1550

Illustration 8: Operating Data Table

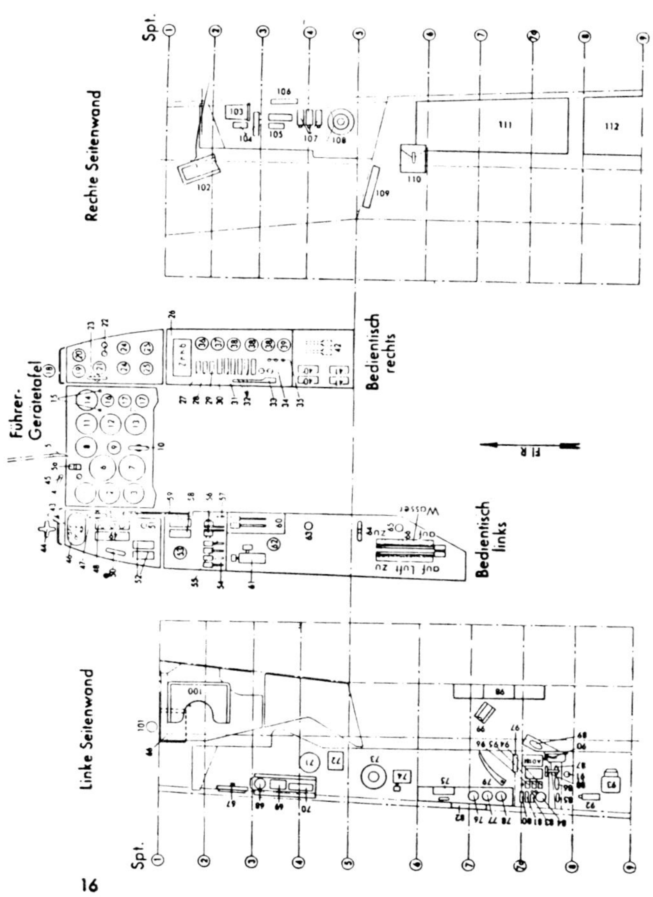

1. Airspeed indicator
2. Fine-coarse altimeter
3. Emergency turn-and-bank indicator
4. Pilot visual indicator
5. Windscreen wiper
6. Turn-and-bank indicator combined with artificial horizon
7. Repeater compass
8. Vertical speed (rate of climb) indicator
9. F 307 indicator
10. Emergency control for windscreen cleaning
11. RPM indicator
12. Boost gauges
13. Fu Ng 101
14. RPM indicator 15.Visual indicator for propeller brake
16. Double propeller position indicator
17. Double pressure gauge
18. Clock
19. Oxygen supply meter
20. Oxygen pressure gauge
21. Rotary switch
22. Coolant level warning
23. Canopy jettison handle
24. Coolant temperature
25. Oil temperature
26. Round counter (ammo)
27. Landing light toggle switch
28. Navigation lights toggle switch
29. UV lighting toggle switch
30. Pitot heat
31. Autopilot master switch
32. Fuel tank pumps
33. Pilot's ejector seat lever
34. Battery switches
35. Fuel level warning
36. Gyro compass control switch
37. Dimmer switch
38. Fuel level gauge
39. Compressed air pressure gauge
40. Starter switches
41. Auxiliary starter switches
42. Fuel emergency jettison levers
43. Undercarriage emergency release handle
44. Nosewheel emergency lowering handle
45. Windscreen washer
46. Indicator light panel (12)
47. Armor shield
48. Landing flaps switch
49. Undercarriage switch
50. Landing flaps emergency lowering lever
51. Electrical system emergency switch
52. Propeller automatic pitch switches
53. Landing flaps indicator
54. Fuel tank switch levers
55. Revolutions correction setting
56. Throttle lever with thumb switch (propeller pitch)
57. Locking lever (undercarriage ground brake)
58. Ignition switch
59. Control surface locking lever
60. Emergency handle for cooling flaps
61. Trimmer
62. Double pressure gauge, hydraulic fluid
63. Accumulator filler
64. Life raft emergency handle
65. Access ladder
66. Heating control
67. Ventilation flap control
68. Dimmer switch
69. Intercom socket
70. Controls for FuG 17 (radio set)
71. Fuse for demolition charge
72. Plug-in for heated flight suit
73. Radio operator's oxygen supply
74. Plug-in for heated flight suit
75. Destruct switch for radio equipment
76. Outside air temperature gauge
77. Oxygen pressure gauge
78. Oxygen supply meter
79. Observer's ejector seat lever80 Selector switch FuG10,FuG 16
81. "Measure Range" toggle switch
82. Kärcher heater operating data plate
83. UV lighting toggle switch
84. Compressed air pressure gauge
85. Volt-Amp meter
86. Altimeter
87. Dimmer
88. Canopy jettison
89. Airspeed indicato
90. Transmitter key FuG 10
91. Trailing antenna jettison
92. Rheostat
93. Resistance box
94. Propeller de-icing toggle switch
95. Wing heating (de-ice) toggle switch
96. Wing heating (de-ice) toggle switch
97. Hand lamp
98. Flare box
99. Flare pistol rack
100. Map case
101. Intercom external plug-in
102. Deviation chart
103. Emergency compass
104. UV lights
105. Instrument lighting
106. Operating data plate for ejector seat system
107. UV lighting rheostats
108. Pilot's oxygen supply
109. Electrical distributing board
110. First-aid kit
111. Main switchboard
112. Space for radio distributing board

Illustration 3: Instrument Overview (Cockpit)

11. Dimensions

Wingspan	18.5 m
Length	15.54 m
Height	4.4 m
Wheel base	5 m
Wing area	44.5 m²
Wing loading at weight of 12.2 tons	275 kg/m²

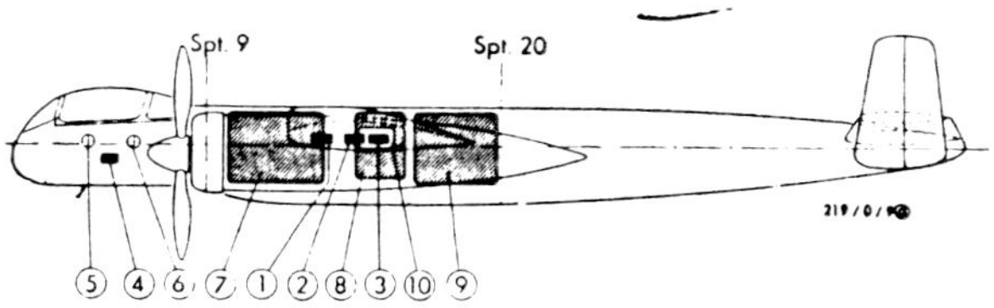

12. Loading Chart

Night Fighter	Position	Designation kg
	Empty Weight +/- 1.5% tolerance	8490
	Additional Equipment	1080
	Equipped Weight	9570
1	Ammunition for fuselage weapons, forward, 600 rounds	134
2	Ammunition for fuselage weapons, center section, 600 rounds	134
3	Ammunition for wing weapons, 600 rounds	134
4	Flares	2
5	Pilot	100
6	Observer	100
7	Fuel in forward tank, 1100 liters	820
8	Fuel in middle tank, 500 liters	370
9	Fuel in rear tank, 1000 liters	735
10	Lubricating oil, 2 x 90 liters	160
	Loaded Weight	12260

Center of gravity distance in meters behind datum plane	
Undercarriage extended	5.683
Undercarriage retracted	5.733
CG Position in % tg:	
Undercarriage extended	28.4
Undercarriage retracted	30.4

Note:
a.This loading chart is valid only for a fully-equipped aircraft (see loading instructions).

b.**Maximum allowable gross weight = 12350 kg**

c.Installation of a trailing antenna in the fuselage tail raises gross weight by approx. 20 kg, CG position moves aft by 0.5%.

See also loading file and Part 8 F "Modification Kits" of the Aircraft Handbook

13. Loading Instructions

Normal loading situations are contained in the loading chart. For unforeseen special cases, determine the new CG position from the weight and moment table and ascertain whether the new value falls within the allowable limits. An example of a CG calculation is provided at the end of the loading instructions. In compiling the loading plan it is assumed that all elements of standard airframe and engine equipment are installed. If the removal of individual parts becomes necessary, determine the weight and position of these parts and calculate the effect on the CG position.

Moment point: (see loading chart)
Moment arm x relative to axis of reference = 6 m in front of main spar
Allowable CG positions:
18.0%+31.5% = 5.414+5.763 m behind datum plane

Most forward CG position for a normally-equipped aircraft:

23.4% = 5.553 m behind datum plane

This occurs with the undercarriage extended when fuel tanks and ammunition containers are empty.

SECRET

Memorandum

Subject: He 219 – Visit to Venlo on 30.5.43

Among the gentlemen present:

General Kammhuber (General Commanding Night Fighters)
Oberst Peltz (Commander of the air war against England)
General Vorwald
Oberst von Lossberg
Major Streib
Oberleutnant Meurer
Oberleutnant Haussdorff
Director Francke
Hilber
Meschkat

1. Course of the Inspection

General Kammhuber and his guests arrived for lunch at 1:30 P.M. Afterward the He 219 V 7, which was parked on the airfield, was given a thorough inspection. The aircraft did not fly.

At about 3 P.M. General Vorwald and Oberst von Lossberg flew to Southern France. General Kammhuber and the rest of the guests continued on by car. We ourselves arrived on Saturday evening, 29.5.43, and flew back to Rostock on Sunday at 6 P.M.

2. Assessment of the He 219 During the Inspection

The officers liked the machine very much. Oberst Peltz said that it was the first really uncompromising aircraft. The aircrews stated that the He 219's great endurance, between 4 and 5 hours at low throttle settings, was its most significant advantage. This will increase downings of enemy aircraft considerably, especially by the good pilots. At present with the Me 110 one must land again after one hour and forty minutes, often when there are still plenty of opportunities for victories or when enemy incursions are just beginning. The He 219 will retain its advantage of greater endurance compared to the Focke-Wulf Ta 154 night fighter and the Me 410, should this be considered for the night fighter role.

3. Brake

It was requested that consideration be given to a speed brake installation as this is very desirable. It often occurs that a night fighter is holding at a height of 8 kilometers and is then sent after an enemy at 2 kilometers. It is then important to lose height as quickly as possible. The brake is also desirable in order to reduce overtaking speed when closing with the enemy.

Director Francke pointed out that considerable drag is produced by the propeller automatic pitch mechanism when the throttles are closed, so that the automatic pitch mechanism makes the brake unnecessary.

4. Emergency Fuel Jettisoning

Director Francke reported that it had been decided to reintroduce fuel jettisoning in spite of the aircraft's good single-engine characteristics, in order to provide the crews with even better handling at maximum gross weight and possibly even allow them to avoid forced landings. General Kammhuber declared himself to be very much in agreement, however he declared that he would not change the order to carry out a forced landing in the event of the loss of one engine. The emergency fuel jettisoning would, however, contribute to making landings less dangerous and limit damage to the aircraft.

5. First Night Fighter Mission

General Kammhuber decided that the He 219 V 9 would initially be used on operations, flown by Major Streib. It is expected that the mission will take place in the week of the 2nd to the 5th of June. If the first operational flights produced positive results, the V 9 was to be employed in a newly-created zone for the ZE (Y) radio equipment. The Y-System enables better control from the ground.

The V 7 is not to be used initially.

7. Nosewheel Testing

There is much interest as to how the aircraft would behave without a nosewheel. Director Francke proposed an experiment when more machines are available.

8. Propeller Automatic Pitch Control

Oberst von Lossberg intends to step in to see to it that priority is given to delivering engines for the He 219 with the propeller automatic pitch mechanism.

9. Shortage of Engines

Here too Oberst von Lossberg will step in to see to it that we receive the first ten engines from Daimler-Benz's June production. According to information already provided by Staff Engineer Bosse, a further ten engines are supposed to be en route to Vienna from Oberpfaffenhofen.

10. Oberpfaffenhofen for the Production He 219

During the conversation with Staff Engineer Bosse, Director Francke came up with the idea of proposing Oberpfaffenhofen as a further production site for the He 219, as information received indicated that the Do 217 was being dropped for good as an unnecessary type. Production in Oberpfaffenhofen is listed as 20 Do 217s per month. Director von Pfistermeister will pursue this proposal through Director Frydag.

11. Courier Aircraft for General Kammhuber

General Kammhuber would very much like to obtain an He 219 for himself as a courier aircraft in the near future. At the present time consideration is being given to producing this courier version from one of the prototypes.

12. Repeater Compass

Oberleutnant Hausdorff carried out an experimental installation with a larger instrument. All participants characterized it as extremely good. Approximately 150 instruments are supposed to be still available. Venlo can convert the first machines itself. Oberst von Lossberg is clearing the release of the available instruments for the He 219.

The very successful Knight's Cross wearer, Oberleutnant Meurer, who was supposed to have this machine, is deeply grieved. General Kammhuber promised him that he will receive the next one as quickly as possible and he is therefore very interested in soon receiving the V 10, which Director Francke informed us is already flying. Questioned as to further delivery dates, Director Francke stated that it was expected that V 11 and V 12 would be delivered before the end of June. Furthermore, on the basis of the promised skilled workers, which are now on their way, we are endeavoring to increase production to ten a month as ordered.

6. More Careful Repair Shop Work

The Streib group has had to deal with numerous breakdowns in both the radio and electrical systems resulting from grounding. Oberleutnant Hausdorf related that they had recovered a handful of plate nuts and other metal bits from the bottom of the junction box.

Efforts must be made to obtain the more powerful vacuum cleaner, which is available somewhere.

The Streib group felt obliged to mention this complaint in passing, because the question had been directed at Major Streib as to why the aircraft had not seen action yet even though they arrived on
May 12.

> Note: The fact that the aircraft has not yet seen action is because of familiarization of the crew and ground personnel with the aircraft, and a certain amount of daylight testing has already taken place.

During the inspection General Vorwald spoke of several complaints, to which the firm must pay particular attention when delivering the next machines. Vorwald's attitude was in no way reproachful, rather he and the other officers acknowledged that the firm had made every effort to do its best and promptly meet its deadlines.

As they will be significantly more critical with the next machines, it is doubly important to avoid all the complaints that have arisen through special checks. Herr Hilber, who will be in Vienna in the next days, is the best informed concerning the details.

13. Airspeed Indicator for the Radio Operator

This is considered indispensable for operational reasons and must be added. The pilot can concentrate on observing outside the aircraft while the radio operator relays aircraft speed to him.

14. Desired Replacement Parts

An armor shield and the plexiglass hood in front of it are urgently requested for the V 9. Also requested are replacement tires.

signed Meschkat

Distribution:
Prof. Dr. Heinkel
Dir. Francke
Dir. Schaberger
Schwärzler
Kapp
Raue
Hilber
BB

– –

Translated from the German by David Johnston.
Front cover artwork by Steve Ferguson, Colorado Springs, CO.

This title was originally published by Flugzeug Publikations GmbH.

Library of Congress Catalog Number: 95-67545

Printed in China.
ISBN: 0-88740-819-2

Published by Schiffer Publishing Ltd.
77 Lower Valley Road
Atglen, PA 19310
Please write for a free catalog.
This book may be purchased from the publisher.
Please include $2.95 postage.
Try your bookstore first.